# BOOTS RILEY

# BOOTS RILEY

## TELL HOMELAND SECURITY— WE ARE THE BOMB

CHICAGO

Published by Haymarket Books
PO Box 180165
Chicago, IL 60618
773-583-7884
info@haymarketbooks.org
www.haymarketbooks.org

ISBN: 978-1-60846-253-7

In the US, through Consortium Book Sales and Distribution, www.cbsd.com
In Canada, Publishers Group Canada, www.pgcbooks.ca
In the UK, Turnaround Publisher Services, www.turnaround-uk.com
All other countries, Publishers Group Worldwide, www.pgw.com

This book was published with the generous support of the Wallace Action Fund and Lannan Foundation.
Discounts on bulk purchases are available from Haymarket Books for organizations, teachers, activists, and others.
Please contact info@haymarketbooks.org for more information.

Cover and design by Ragina Johnson.
Cover image of Boots in Niort, France, during the "Jeudis de Niort" festival on July 24, 2014, by and courtesy of Jean-Freetz.

Library of Congress CIP Data is available.

10 9 8 7 6 5 4 3 2 1

Photo credits
Eric Arnold: 8 (bottom inset)
Todd Cooper (jasontoddcooper.com): 30, 32–33, 104–105
The Coup: 42 (main photo)
Cory Dewald: 8 (top inset), 10 (main image), 11 (right page, top inset), 12 (insets), 68, 98
James Fassinger: 39
Auintard Henderson: 131
IMPS of MARGE and FLETCH: 16 (album cover photo), 46
Amelia Kennedy: frontis, 11 (right page, bottom inset)
Larisa Mann: 200 (right inset)

Matt Reamer: 200 (center inset)
Boots Riley: 192
Rasheed Shabazz: 25
Jake Stangel: 75, 110–111, 112 (main photo)
Street Sweeper Social Club: 209, 210, 226
Romy Suskin: 47
Haymarket Books has sought to identify all copyright holders for all images included in this book. If you feel your work was included here and not properly credited, please contact us.

*This is for my folkers who got bills overdue*

# CONTENTS

"FOR BOOTS, A SLICK SIMILE, A CLEVER PUNCH LINE, IS NEVER ITS OWN REWARD. HIS SONGS ARE SOUNDTRACKS TO THE STRUGGLE— NOT SUBSTITUTES FOR IT, LIKE SO MUCH 'CONSCIOUS' HIP-HOP HAS BECOME."

Main photo: "Me at age one. I'm sure the book wasn't a standard prop at the Sears portrait studio at which this was taken." — BOOTS

# FOREWORD

## BY ADAM MANSBACH

**I FIRST MET BOOTS RILEY AT STANFORD UNIVERSITY IN 2006; HE AND I WERE SPEAKING ON DIFFERENT PANELS AT A HIP-HOP CONFERENCE.** I can't recall the topic of mine, but Boots's was entitled "I Am Hip-Hop: The Artist as Theorist," and it featured a staggeringly long and ill-considered soliloquy by KRS-One, whose personal beef with another panelist quickly metastasized into an open-ended harangue, no less deeply felt for the absence of any real objective. A series of attempts to guide The Blastmaster to a gentle landing failed, and the farce dragged on until his mic was cut off, at which point KRS and his entourage bounced.

When the smoke cleared, Boots did what he does: leaned low over a microphone and made crazy sense, cutting through hours of bullshit with seconds of stark lucidity. The essence of his opening statement was this: *I rhyme because it's what the people I want to reach want to hear. If folks were into country music, I'd do that.* Moments later, somebody whispered something in his ear, and Boots

took off. Turned out the afternoon's drama had affected his son Xola, who was attending in utero, and dude decided it was time to be born.

Nine years later, those words still resonate in my mind. Boots's sentiment stood in contrast to more than the tenor of the day's proceedings: it was, and remains, impossible to imagine any other MC of his caliber making such a declaration. This is not to say that Boots doesn't bleed hip-hop, or that he's unique in making music with a message; on the contrary, The Coup can trace their lineage back to the populist anthems of Pete Seeger, the sly, incisive commentary of Gil Scott-Heron, the social realism of Melle Mel, the storytelling prowess of Slick Rick, the history-freighted agitprop of Public Enemy.

But in an industry built on ego, Boots has made a career of self-effacement—of working for something bigger than fame, and bigger than hip-hop; the fact that he left music entirely for several years in order to cofound The Young Comrades is proof enough of that. It's never been all about him,

and therein lies the power and the problem. A movement that can't be destroyed by cutting off the leader's head is a strong one; a rap group whose name is always preceded by epithets like "political" and "radical" seldom gets discussed in terms of pure aesthetics. Or played on the radio.

And thus, Boots's poetic prowess has been hiding in plain sight for more than twenty years. If he penned battle raps, or if the stories he dropped over beats (beats that are hard; beats that are funky) glamorized conspicuous consumption instead of critiquing it, he'd be on everybody's list of the funniest motherfuckers in the game. But it's damn near impossible to find a self-aggrandizing stanza in The Coup's entire canon—think about that for a second, and then think about the rest of hip-hop.

The most quotable nugget of wordplay on the most recent album illustrates the point. *We got hella people/they got helicopters,* Boots raps. Ninety-five out of a hundred MCs wouldn't have thought of that . . . and four of the remaining five would have flipped it

in reverse, and bragged about having helicopters, gone with hyperbolic braggadocio instead of collective resistance. I know the last thing Boots wants is to be part of the one percent, but there it is.

"The day of the L.A. riots I learned that it meant nothing to be a poet," Paul Beatty once wrote. "One had to be a poet and a farmer, a poet and a roustabout, a poet and a soon-to-be revolutionary." And for Boots, a slick simile, a clever punch line, is never its own reward. His songs are soundtracks to the struggle—not substitutes for it, like so much "conscious" hip-hop has become. His proudest musical accomplishment? The fact that when a group of Native youth turned back an illegal police raid in an eight-hour armed standoff a few years back, they were bumping *Genocide and Juice* the whole time. (Note to audiobook producer: cue the DJ to scratch in Chuck D's "who gives a fuck about a goddamn Grammy" line here.)

The book you're holding contains two decades' worth of songs—an impressive run by any standard, and an epic one in a hip-hop industry determined to herd grown folks off the stage so as to usher in the next generation of exploitable teenagers striking b-boy poses in the wings. *Boots Riley: Tell Homeland Security—We Are the Bomb* is Boots as you've never experienced him: as agate type on bound paper. Reading lyrics sometimes feels like a failed exercise in legitimization: the words just sit there, stripped of the flow that animates them, the beats they were created to ride. It's like going to a graffiti art show, and realizing every single piece would look better rumbling through the city on the side of a train than it does hanging on a wall.

Sometimes, though—and by sometimes, I mean here—a different dynamic asserts itself. Sometimes the MC's flow is hard-wired into his rhymes so profoundly that the bounce, the head nod, the stick-and-move-around-the-pocket remain intact. Airlifted out of their natural habitat, the couplets thrive in captivity. Stripped of their musical armor, a new structural integrity reveals itself; fresh entendres flare out from the page. Like a burner-covered subway car pulling into a station, the whole thing stops moving long enough for us to appreciate just what the fuck is going on.

– ADAM MANSBACH
BERKELEY, CALIFORNIA
MAY 2015

Main photo: "These were standard tools of my first three albums. I used an Atari computer and some software that was very out of date. Often it took me forty-five minutes to start the computer, allowing me time to come up with excuses to not work on music that day." — BOOTS

Left page, insets: Boots at a rally in San Francisco for Mumia Abu-Jamal.

This page inset: Boots at Chub Studio in Oakland, California.

# "BEFORE I WANTED TO BE A REVOLUTIONARY, I WANTED TO BE PRINCE."

BOOTS RILEY

12

Main image: "Me and my younger brother Manuel in my mother's apartment in Oakland. Circa 1981." —BOOTS

Insets: Boots, chair Yana Kuchinoff, and Kevin Coval at Socialism conference session on June 28, 2012.

# INTRO-DUCTION
## MUSIC AND STRUGGLE

This is an edited excerpt of a session with Boots Riley, interviewed by Kevin Coval, at the Socialism conference in Chicago on June 28, 2012.

*One of the things we're going to talk about, especially at the top, is how you became you, if that's fair. So I just want to talk about early influences and [you] being born into a family of activists. What were some of your earliest memories of politics, of movement building?*
Well, the thing that I carried away from the experience of my family being organizers was something that I didn't see as political, but it was that our house always had people in it, and there were always parties—things that later I found out were meetings. There were parties and there would be bid whist games and all that sort of stuff going on.

So when I became an organizer, I felt like the landscape of organizing looked pretty boring. At the time, there would be a lot of demonstrations of five people with picket signs, a study group, or whatever. And I think that glimpse of organizing in Detroit

gave me a vision that it's going to have to be more social. People are going to have to look at it as their own thing in order for them to want to be involved.

*The music entered the picture there, I guess, right? You said parties. I imagine there was music.*
Oh, yeah, yeah, definitely. And I realized that that was culture. There was a culture being built around that. Of course, some of what I know about it is from asking questions later, but I realized that it is important to have fun and make people understand that these ideas are about how to live life in a more comfortable way. That there is a struggle, but that struggle not only will make your life fulfilled once this inevitable revolution that may happen sometime in the future happens, but it will make your life better right now, and that engaging with other folks is a better way of living.

*We're going to come back to that intersection of art and culture and politics and fun. But I*

*want to go back to music. You produce a lot of The Coup records, so I'm curious about early influences sonically. Who were you digging as a kid or what are some of the first records that you remember hearing that made you want to explore more or dig for records?*

Prince was probably the first. Before I wanted to be a revolutionary, I wanted to be Prince.

*And The Revolution.*
That was part of this yearning that I see in a lot of young kids, that they wish they were on TV. That was me. They wish they were performing. And it comes out of this idea that we're not important and those are the important people. Some of it comes out of that idea. We see these folks that really affect us emotionally, and we want to be part of that, we want to do that, too. We don't want to be insignificant. And I think that later, when I became an organizer, I was able to get that feeling of having some meaning and being part of it all, being part of the world and not being passed over. I think that those things

are very much connected. Many of us are told at some point, either through example or whatever, that we don't have the time or we shouldn't be an artist. And I think that it is something inherent in humanity to create. And we don't have the time, we really don't. Many of us have to survive and spend most of our time doing that.

*When did you start making stuff?*
I started out writing in high school.

*What got you started? Literature or hip-hop?*
A teacher getting me to write stories. Then the drama club needed someone to write a version of *West Side Story*, so even though I didn't rap, I wrote a rap version of *West Side Story* that was based in Oakland called *East Side Story*. Actually, the woman, now woman, who worked on it with me ended up being the star in *Heaven and Earth*.

*You don't remember any of the verses from East Side Story?*
No. But because people didn't boo it—

*That was encouragement.*
—I was, like, Oh, I can do this.

*So you wrote it in rap, but you weren't rhyming at the time.*
No. Everybody was. It was something that you just did around town. It wasn't even a competition for us in the sense that none of us really—there were a couple people that we thought were really good. One was my friend Johnny. But if you weren't one of those couple people, you just rapped. You beat on tables at lunchtime. It was just something everybody did.

*But this isn't the emergence of that moment, right? Prior to your teenage years, hip-hop wasn't prevalent because it didn't exist, right, in the sense that it gets to the Bay Area in, what, the late '70s, early '80s, at the earliest?*
Okay, here's the thing. I don't subscribe to the common hip-hop narrative that hip-hop started because somebody put the peanut butter in the chocolate in the Bronx somewhere on one particular night. It didn't hap-

pen that way. When hip-hop came in the form that it is right now, Black people didn't say, "Wow, what is this new thing? It's ingenious." It was something that was already part of the culture. And I think that history is taught in that way, that it happened from these particular instances, is one that takes hip-hop and tries to separate it from the Black experience. And by doing so, it looks at it in a vacuum that is separate from the history of Black people, which is a history of struggle.

So to prove my point, when I lived in Detroit, my older brother and his friends would all do hambone—and I can't do it—beat on their chests and on their legs and slap. They would rap against each other. This was in the mid-seventies in Detroit. Nobody was calling it hip-hop or anything like that, but it was something that was done. I hear people from Newark talking about in the '70s maybe that there were all these mattresses around, and it was a big thing to flip on mattresses to music. That's why you hear in Lauryn Hill's "Everything [Is Everything]," she says "Flippin' in the ghetto on a dirty mattress." It became an art form and a sport. However, it didn't happen in other places and it wasn't included in hip-hop. Neither was hamboning.

But when I moved to Oakland and the first time I heard Sugarhill Gang, there was somebody else from the Midwest or the South, and we both said, "They're playing a hambone song on the radio." And there is a recorded collection of songs from prisons from the '30s, '40s, '50s, and '60s called *Get Your Ass in the Water and Swim Like Me*, and they're rapping on that. In 1963, there was a top-ten song on the radio called "Here Comes the Judge," by Pigmeat Markham. Listen to it. It sounds more like a Sugarhill record than Sugarhill records did.

*And Langston Hughes was rhyming over blues. Yes, there's a long, long tradition.*
Yes. Also, when you're a kid, three years is a long time. So by this time we're talking about the late '80s. So if somebody told us that hip-hop was new, we wouldn't have thought that.

*But you started rhyming in high school, or prior to that.*
Just for fun, yes.

*When did you start to take it more seriously as a craft?*
Well, there is a particular—I come from an organization that was pretty sectarian and didn't look at culture in the way that, let's say, I look at it now, and maybe even that organization looks at it now. Culture that was created by capitalism was not looked at as something that could be used for revolutionary purposes. However, one, I didn't care, because I like music, I'm going to like what I like; and, two, I was also looking for ways to put these ideas out in large ways.

There was a thing that happened. We were canvassing this area of San Francisco called Double Rock, and we would do that every week. There were a few struggles going on there that we were involved in. But something happened in between the two weekly visits that we made, and this was very important in my realization of what could happen with hip-hop.

A woman named Rossy Hawkins and her two twin sons who were eight years old got beat down, bloodied by the police in the Double Rock projects. The neighborhood immediately came out, hundreds of people, and surrounded the police. What had happened a week or two before was a guy had gotten beaten up by the police and been taken in the police car and driven around until he died—because they didn't take him to the hospital. So people wanted to get Rossy and her kids away from the police and take her to the hospital because they feared for her life. So they surrounded the police, and the police got scared and started shooting up in the air. If you've ever been around a gun going off, you know that whatever you were thinking a second before is not what you're thinking then. You're thinking, Let me get the fuck out of here. And everybody ran away. But at a certain point everybody turned around. They turned around and came back, got Rossy and her kids away from the police, and sent those police out without their car. The car was turned over.

So two things. One, none of this was put in any mainstream newspapers or anything like that the next day. What I've told you so far is what dozens of people said. Other folks added other things. But this is what everyone agreed happened, everything that I've told you so far. And the other thing that happened is that what made everyone turn around was this: It was the summer of 1989, and the number-one song on the radio was "Fight the Power" by Public Enemy. And somebody started chanting "Fight the power, fight the power, fight the power." And everyone said that then is when they knew that they all had a job to do.

When that story was being told to me that day is when I realized the power that music could have, that hip-hop could be a rallying cry that consolidates our ideas into action.

*When did you know that you were beginning to act as this person who is making this grand commentary on culture and people were listening?*
I didn't look at it as critiquing the mainstream music that was out at the time. A lot of people make that assumption because our album was called *Genocide and Juice* and Snoop had a song called "Gin and Juice." But gin and juice was a popular drink in the Bay Area way before that song. And actually, he did that song because Spice 1, who is from the Bay Area, always talked about gin and juice. It was just like part of popular culture. So the idea was that the album was a concoction, and we were talking about the genocide that's going on under capitalism as well as giving you some music, which is the juice part of it.

*That's kind of where you live. You referred to it as being someone who is giving you this understanding and making it funky always. That's the signature, it seems, of some of the records that you put out, is that it's conscious and it makes you want to move. It's music that you could not only knock your head to but dance to on some funky, funky . . .*
And for me, I feel like that is one aspect of it, when you hear music that you can't just put into an intellectual box, that makes you move your body. It's funny, my daughter was listen-

ing to "Candy" when she was, like, three, by Cameo. She said, "Daddy, this music is making me dance even though I don't want to." There is something about that, making music that touches you in that way, and combining it with lyrics that encourage you to move your body in the long term in a certain way. That's just been something that I like to combine.

It also has to do with an outlook. A lot of folks who entered into the arena of trying to talk about world affairs or even local politics or whatever was happening came at it from a standpoint of doom and gloom, like, "Everything is fucked up, and you should get angry." Even visual art was like that a lot. You would see, a lot of murals that were radical in their analysis, but they were dark and gloomy, and there was no vision of what could happen. I think that for me the slow, head-nodding beat didn't do it. It didn't allow for that hopefulness. And it comes with an analysis that things will change once there's a mass movement that gets rid of this system. So I think that a lot of music came to the doom-and-gloom aesthetic because there was no movement giving that other analysis. There was a yearning for things to be different . . .

I was doing a workshop at La Peña Cultural Center, which is actually, I think, technically in Berkeley. This was at the time of the campaign against Prop 21, which was a proposition that, among other things, would allow fourteen-year-olds to be sentenced to prison as adults and also defined a gang as three people wearing similar clothing. So we did a campaign against this. It was an art and organizing workshop. What we did was we got a whole bunch of people together and had everybody write about this, and we put out a free cassette that was like a newspaper on tape talking about this issue. And we got on a flatbed truck and went around to neighborhoods and did concerts and gave out the cassettes. It was more of an experiment to see how to use hip-hop in organizing.

*You also use not only funk and fun, but also humor seems to be an important part of the work that you do you as an artist. The "5 Million Ways to Kill a CEO" joint, for instance, is pretty fuckin' funny. So how does that find its*

*way into your work? I would imagine that is also an important aspect, to bring that to the organizing work as well.*
I think there's a couple of things. Some of the first organizers I was around were like old-school union folks and old-school CP folks from the '50s. They had some experience in organizing their peers, and they had some success. And they were always the funny dudes. They were always the people who could engage in a conversation, see the irony in what was being talked about, point that out, and be funny. They also were often—one guy that I came up around was this old English dude that had done union work in England, and he was always, like, "If you can't share a pint with somebody, how are you going to expect them to go on strike with you?"

*Yes, human shit.*
So I always made the connection that it's really about—it's not just about you giving someone some facts and figures. It's about people relating to you as a human being. And then they can relate to your thought processes. So that's some of it. But I think it wasn't as thought out as that. When I used to think of myself as more of one of those lyricists, writers, whatever, that I actually try to get away from, it was kind of like the lines that we thought were witty and cool were based on some sort of irony that was humorous.

A lot of times when I'm writing my lyrics, I realize that they may be seen before they're heard. So it definitely influences my writing. I like the way certain words look more than other words, or I like how this sort of break in the line fits. There definitely have been choices that I've made because of that.

*Poetry.*
So I've always wanted to put out my lyrics in print. And there are stories about how certain songs came to be and the making of certain songs—just talking about the same kind of stuff I'm talking about right now.

# SORRY TO BOTHER YOU (2012)

1.  THE MAGIC CLAP
2.  STRANGE ARITHMETIC
3.  YOUR PARENTS' COCAINE
4.  THE GODS OF SCIENCE
5.  MY MURDER, MY LOVE
6.  YOU ARE NOT A RIOT (AN RSVP FROM DAVID SIQUEIROS TO ANDY WARHOL)
7.  LAND OF 7 BILLION DANCES
8.  VIOLET
9.  THIS YEAR*
10. WE'VE GOT A LOT TO TEACH YOU, CASSIUS GREEN
11. LONG ISLAND ICED TEA, NEAT
12. THE GUILLOTINE
13. WAVIP

*This song appears here with additional lyrics.

# SORRY TO BOTHER YOU, THE MOVIE

A lot of times I need reasons to do things and I didn't exactly know what I wanted to do with the next Coup album, so instead of writing an album I wrote a script.

The script is a dark comedy with magical realism and science fiction inspired by my time as a telemarketer. It's called *Sorry to Bother You*—which is also the name of the album. I wrote the script and then I worked on the album that goes with it, and I purposely made it so that you could listen to the album and the songs without needing to know what's going on in the movie. Because I wrote the script not knowing how, if, or whether the movie would be made. The music and the songs are inspired by different things that happen in the movie or their emotional equivalents, but I'm writing songs that have to do with something else outside of it, too. In this case, we had to put the album out—I finished the album and the movie wasn't ready. Now the movie is being made. We've got a great producing team and San Francisco Film Society is helping out. We've got Wyatt Cenac, Patton Oswalt, and David Cross on board. You'll know, and you'll get to hear, the songs in context. I wanted them both to exist on their own; I just needed a creative center point to go from. I like The Who, I mean I like *Tommy* and I like *The Wall*, and I think there are a lot of ways that what we did on this album reminds me of *The Wall*, like a lot of the kids chanting and things like that definitely were influenced by it. — BOOTS

*The description of songs—along with the anecdotes contained herein— were transcribed from audio recordings of conversations with Boots Riley.*

# THE MAGIC CLAP

"The Magic Clap" is that sound that happens at the moment when thought leads to action. So it's supposed to represent that quantitative to qualitative leap, that's kind of what it's talking about. Songwriting-wise it's what I was doing in this whole album, which is less relying on some of the tools that are known to a lot of lyricists—simile, metaphor, and maybe puns. I think that those are interesting tools, and I used them a lot and got really bored with them and they start feeling like just cartwheels and tricks. With this album I wanted to feel more like a songwriter. Especially in the last verse of this song, it's where I was going with that. The actual song was created on the day that I got together with my current girlfriend who I have a child with now, and we wrote that song together. She played the accordion on it and we came up with that in the studio and the energy of the song is there. So the first verse of the song is actually about exactly what I said the song is about, but it's also a romantic song. A lot of things that get me excited about

## THE MAGIC CLAP

It's like a hotwire, baby,
when we put it together
when the sparks fly
we'll ignite the future forever
this is the last kiss martin ever gave to coretta
it's like a paparazzi picture when i flash my beretta
i got scars on my back
the truth on my tongue
i had the money in my hand when that alarm got rung
we wanna breathe fire and freedom from our lungs
tell homeland security
we are the bomb

hurry up, get in, close the do'
this here the meeting for the overthrow
waitin on that concrete rose to grow
doin lines that aint quotable
countin up all that dough you owe
you aint sposed to know it's opposable
we are not disposable
muscle up kid
we got blows to throw
til the folks have risen
there'll be no decision
we make the motor move
they chauffeur driven
right now we can't shine right like a broken prism
i figured out the 14th is a broke amendment
good evening
tonight we bring to you
worn out streets that'll sing to you
.45 shells that'll dance to the beats
stomachs so loud it'll cancel the speech
checks that vanish if you blink an eye
grace gettin locked in the clink to die
a salary cap on a birth certificate
notarized lies that burst in triplicate
morning prayers for the car to start
a man and a whiskey in a heart-to-heart
hope in a track suit to flash and run
while agony chases with a badge and gun
poetry shouted from the squeal of the bus breaks
hands in the air try to feel for an escape
flash in my eyes like candid snaps
when we slap back it's the magic clap

Stills captured from video for "The Magic Clap," featuring
Patton Oswalt, directed and edited by Pete Lee, 2012.

writing are things that get me excited about life. They're very intertwined and if I try to separate them, then songs just sound mechanical. So I've learned to not try to guide them too much except in a general way and try to feed the energy that's already there. The Patton Oswalt video for the song came together because he was tweeting Coup lyrics and people started tweeting me, "Patton Oswalt is tweeting your lyrics." So I started talking with him. Earlier on while we were promoting, he said, "What can I do to help you?" And I said, well as a matter of fact, you can help do this video and Pete Lee, the guy who directed the original "Magic Clap" video, a good friend of mine, he came up with this idea and it just sounded like a winner.

The idea is that Patton is doing an ultra-literal translation of the song. A visual translation of the lyrics and he's not only taking each word and doing an action that represents what that word means to him, but he's also taking words and breaking the syllables down into actions that represent words that those syllables sound like. So let me think of an example: *salary* becomes *celery* or something, you know there's a couple ones that are multisyllabic that he changes into a few words. Patton would take words like *broken* and make it two words: *bro* as in the stereotypical white sports guy fan, frat boy, bro Oswalt—he'd act like that—and then *Ken*, a Ken doll. And so doing this and putting all those images back to back made for a hilarious montage that even now when I just looked at it a few seconds ago, I'm catching things that I didn't, that my eye didn't notice before. He just basically said, "How can I help the world know more about The Coup?" He came out at like six in the morning, worked for free for like four or five hours and left us to go do some other gig. He's a pretty cool dude. — BOOTS

Still captured from video for "The Magic Clap," featuring Patton Oswalt, directed and edited by Pete Lee, 2012.

# "HE'S ALSO TAKING WORDS AND BREAKING THE SYLLABLES DOWN INTO ACTIONS THAT REPRESENT WORDS."

# STRANGE ARITHMETIC

"Stills from the video for 'Strange Arithmetic.' Directed by a group of ten- to twelve-year-olds as part of the OMG 'Cameras Everywhere' film camp." — BOOTS

This song is about the difference between knowledge and analysis and it talks about how the school system as it exists now usually gives us a bunch of facts with an incorrect analysis. It has us using our education in ways that aren't helpful to us or humanity and also gives us a skewed view of the world because education as it stands stays away from having a class analysis. **So that's basically what this is encouraging. You know, a lot of my development came from a few really good teachers and some of them weren't my teachers, they just happened to be teachers who wanted to educate kids about how this system works, and I also just happen to have friends who are teachers and they're always just coming up with the problem between their politics and what they are legally allowed to say in class. So this is encouraging all those teachers to say look, this is the right thing to do. You are giving people a real education if you are giving them a class analysis. This is actually a song that I had originally written for Street Sweeper Social Club but we never finished. — BOOTS**

# STRANGE ARITHMETIC

History has taught me some strange arithmetic
Using swords, prison bars, and pistol grips
English is the art of bombing towns
While assuring that you really only blessed the ground
Science is that honorable, useful study
Where you contort the molecules and then you make that money
In mathematics, dead children don't get added
But they count the cost of bullets comin out the automatic

Teacher
My hands up
Please, don't make me a victim
Teachers
Stand up
You need to tell us how to flip this system

Economics is the symphony of hunger and theft
Mortar shells often echo out the cashing of checks
In Geography class, it's borders, mountains and rivers
But they will never show the line between the takers and givers
Algebra is that unique occasion
In which a school can say that there should be a balanced equation
And then Statistics is the tool of the complicit
To say everybody's with it and that you're the only critic

Teacher
My hands up
Please, don't make me a victim
Teachers
Stand up
You need to tell us how to flip this system

Social Studies, the goliath to tackle
Which turns into a sermon on simplicity of shackles
Physics is to school you on the science of force
'Cept for how to break the hell out the ghetto, of course
Home Ec can teach you how to make a few sauces
And accept low pay from your Walmart bosses
If your school won't show you how to fight for what's needed
Then they're training you to go through life and get cheated

Teacher
My hands up
Please, don't make me a victim
Teachers
Stand up
You need to tell us how to flip this system

# YOUR PARENTS' COCAINE

So a lot of times when I'm writing a song I'll make the music first, make music that I like and then listen to it and figure out what emotional point that music brings me to, and then I'll go from there and be at that emotional point and figure out what ideas I have that are connected to that emotion. **I got a new keyboard, which is a Little Phatty, a Moog keyboard, but a newer one. And I messed around and I came up with what ends up being the main line of the song and it was on the Moog keyboard, but it sounded real squishy and farty like a kazoo, and so as we were making it, we said that sounds like a kazoo, so let's just throw kazoos in there.**

**At that point, once it got to that sort of silly level, it made me think of, I don't know why, a Billy Joel song. I don't know why my mind works that way, but maybe it had something to do with the pianos that we put on there.**

## YOUR PARENTS' COCAINE

The valet pointed me through the door
One more shot and you're on the floor
If cash talks, yours is a lion's roar
Ghesquière, Christian Dior
You're the asshole ambassador
But your friends obey like Labradors
I vomited on the alpine décor
It's okay, your daddy gon' buy some more

All your friends from school are here
Your frat boys got the rufies near
What will they want when you're out of beer?
Your parents' cocaine!
Your graduation monster bash
The maids will pick up all the trash
In almost every room is stashed
Your parents' cocaine!

Your daddy gon' make you VP of sales
Don't mix good shit with the ginger ale
Pacific Heights ain't Sunnydale
You could murder somebody and be out on bail
Your mom's Amtrak—she's on the rails
So many bumps thought it was Braille
One day, we're all gonna tip the scales
Cuz me and my crew are too big to fail

Steve and Katie shut
the door
And fucked all on the
bathroom floor
Now they're up and looking for
Your parents' cocaine!
Until you get that trust fund check
Pretend you worked for your respect
Janie's asking if she
can test
Your parents' cocaine!

All your esteemed colleagues and guests
Are here to celebrate your success
They only say "Good Luck!" in jest
Your fortune guaranteed at the breast
And Dave, who lets you win at chess
Is with your girlfriend in her dress
They're tired of being your marionettes
You'll mourn in Rio via company jet

Your daddy's got
a business plan
Which made wars
in Afghanistan
It bought your house in Bangkok and
Your parents' cocaine!
Narcos kicked my windows out
They beat and dragged me out the house
They don't give a fuck about
Your parents' cocaine!

"This is a shot from when Occupy Oakland took back the square. This was the front of the march, and these are who OPD was so afraid of that they shot rubber bullets and tear gas." — BOOTS

25

SORRY TO BOTHER YOU (2012)

He sometimes has, he has a few songs in which he's better than the person that he's talking to. I don't have a lot of songs like that, I don't think, unless it's talking about the ruling class, but this song felt more personal.

And while we were making it, I think we had gone to get something to eat and Damion Gallegos, who coproduced the album with me, told a story in which he was talking about being in high school and going to this rich kid's house and saying, "Get out of my way and show me where your parents' cocaine is at." I was like, "That's a song right there." So the song really ends up being about power and inheritance and how power is distributed in this system, how wealth is distributed. Metaphorically it's not even his cocaine; it's his parents' cocaine that people are hanging around him for. We did a fun video, these guys, Eat the Fish, who do crazy videos and are down to do anything, they made up some puppets from found things and we did this. This song is with Anti-Flag and as I made the chorus I was actually thinking of them doing it, I knew they would. So I let my mind go there.

I think that's what I was saying, with some of my work now, once you become known, "Oh he's a good lyricist," it's like you're doing cartwheels and you can do this trick, and you can do that trick. You know, and I listen to rappers that get popular and I can see exactly what they're doing, I can map it out. That's interesting, there's a craftsmanship to that, but it doesn't make me feel anything. People talk about the idea that Tupac had more emotion in his stuff than Biggie. I think what they mean is that he wasn't using a lot of metaphor and simile (what they call "metaphor" when they really mean "simile"), but he wasn't using a lot of that. He was just saying things that were emotionally raw. I think he saw that that's the thing people wanted him to do so he did that.

I think that also, one of the reasons people like his songs more than anything else is because you're so used to these rappers figuring out how to impress you and what to do, and you know that they're not really feeling anything, they're just going to try to impress you. But there's a couple songs like when they're dissing somebody you can tell they feel it. That they were really hurt by something and they want the other person to hurt, so people get attracted to that. Not because the listeners are mean, but finally there is some emotion involved that you can believe.

One of my favorite songs by Kurupt—somebody that is considered a really good rapper—but my favorite song by him—I don't know if he's rhyming at all in it—I think that he found out that his girlfriend Foxy Brown had had an affair with DMX and he makes this whole song where he's just like, *Fuck DMX, fuck the movie* Belly—really, there's not any sense to it except for the fact that you can tell he's really feeling what he's saying.

I think that rap has gotten really, or it's been like that, technical and not a lot of room for emotion. And some of that has to do with the way songs are supposed to be structured, and the way people make their stuff. You go into a studio you hit your sixteen bars. A lot of times I'm listening to songs and it sounds like, I can hear people trying to get to the end. And so with spoken word and other poetry when people say something really poignant, with the same structure, with that same cadence, I can't tell whether they really feel it. I'm not saying I'm right about it, I'm just saying that's how that affects me and that writing didn't. It didn't do that to me.

Stills from the video for "Your Parents' Cocaine" by Eat the Fish Presents. This was filmed at a public access TV studio.

I think that I've definitely been guilty of making—because at first the idea was like, OK, I've got to get this message out. This is what people want. This is the kind of thing that is popular, this is the kind of thing that makes people think I'm a good rapper, so if I do that with this message in there, it will get to them. And I think that that needs to be done, and I think people need to do that. I just think it's at the sacrifice of being the kind of artist you want to be. I think there's a utility to that and people need to keep doing it, but I think that maybe if you can get to a different place and make things that touch you even deeper than that, that maybe people will understand you even more and relate to the general ideas. So that's where I'm going. — BOOTS

Another still from the video for "Your Parents' Cocaine" by Eat the Fish Presents.

ALL YO

"SO THE SONG REALLY ENDS UP BEING ABOUT POWER AND INHERITANCE AND HOW POWER IS DISTRIBUTED IN THIS SYSTEM, HOW WEALTH IS DISTRIBUTED."

FRIENDS FROM SCHOOL ARE HERE

# THE GODS OF SCIENCE

Photo taken in Eugene, Oregon.

**This song has dual origins.** First making it as a recording, I worked with a friend of mine, Bhi Bhiman. He's got this beautiful voice, and he has this other song that I really fell in love with, about the three minutes before Huey Newton got killed—it's him thinking about his life and it's called "Up in Arms." It's just a sad, beautiful song, and I actually heard him singing it in a café. I didn't know who he was and I was like, "OK, I've got to work with you." So he came into the studio and was just messing around with guitar sounds and stuff like that. I already had the idea that I wanted to make this song for two reasons: 1) In the storyline of the movie that I wrote, there is a rich guy who gets these scientists to do things for him and so I wanted to talk about that relationship between capital and science and how science is led by the purse strings. So it's a little bit related to what I talk about in "Strange Arithmetic."

## THE GODS OF SCIENCE

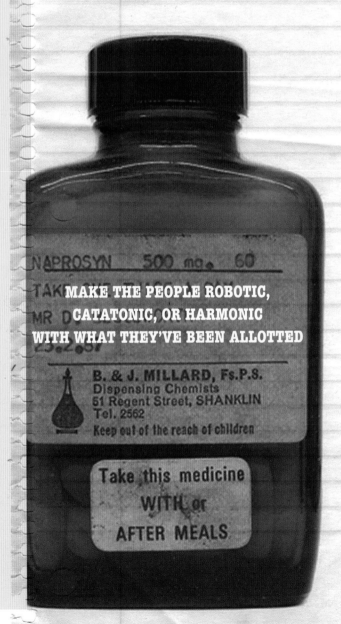

Gods of Science have spoken:
"Grab the wire and choke them"

Hypnotic
The noose is slip-knotted
in a fourth-quarter audit
and pumped through the carotid
Many bought it
Got it in patch, pill, or tonic
Get your credit card
Slot it
And sign it on the dotted
Billionaires have squatted
On the Magna Cum Lauded
Hollered "Take my wallet—
make the people robotic,
catatonic, or harmonic
with what they've been allotted"
And methodically they plotted
Against those who fought it
Whole cities are haunted
Cuz some money bag nodded
And dropped the thought product
Of a Harvard grad upon it
Dollars turn the table—
Boardroom and periodic
Listen to the sonics
Coming through your electronics
You can catalogue it as melodic or atomic
Howsenever, when I bomb it
molecules turn into solids
Some pray to the Christ
Look to Buddha or Mohammed
Some pray to the crack of a rich man's pocket
The biggest advance was plumbing to the projects
Now the scientific process got hijacked for profits
It flows in the direction that a Silver Spoon prodded
We'll get science for the people
When we run the economics

Gods of Science have spoken:
"Grab the wire and choke them"

But I also was thinking about, in terms of my personal life and people that I know, specifically psychotropic medications. It doesn't really get talked about much in the song, but there's all this stuff coming out now that analyzes antidepressants and says, well, there is not really any proof that they actually treat depression and that there has never really been a placebo because everybody that's involved in one of those studies, they know that if they have side effects, they've got the medication and if they don't have side effects, they don't have the medication. So it never worked for people who didn't have the side effects, even if they had the medication. They were able to show some of those things, but also, you know I won't even go into, because that's a long debate, but what they also found is that when they did a meta-analysis of some of these things, what they also discovered was the FDA was allowing some of these drug companies to suppress the various studies that didn't prove that their drug was effective and that other things came out that proved that people like Dr. Drew were getting paid to say that these medications work. Well, there's one situation in which it's been proven that it caused sexual dysfunction, but they were paying Dr. Drew to say that it made people multi-orgasmic and that they also paid journals, medical journals, to have stories in there.

So those were things that were going on in my mind at the time. The song is about how the Gods of Science have spoken. The Gods of Science are the ruling class under this system and the last line is: "We'll get science for the people when we run the economics." So I think that there are probably a lot of really great areas that science could move to, but when it's run by folks who have

"WE JUST NEED TO HAVE A SYSTEM IN WHICH FOOD DOESN'T GET THROWN AWAY, YOU KNOW, AND IN WHICH IT DOESN'T COST MONEY TO BE ABLE TO SURVIVE."

profit as their bottom line or making a more efficient system for profit as their bottom line, we aren't going to explore other areas. I mean, look at everything that we have that we're able to do. The things that we've invented are the things that were in science fiction books when we were kids, and the reason that they've been invented is because they were imagined first in those science fiction books. And why were those things the things that were imagined? It has to do with the way the world was at the time, so when, if there is something that's imagined that could help people share power, if there's something that's imagined that could be of benefit . . . I don't know, some people talk about scientific development that could help feed the world, but we don't really need any scientific development that could help feed the world, we just need to have a system in which food doesn't get thrown away, you know, and in which it doesn't cost money to be able to survive. The "Gods of Science" is about the gods that scientific funders have to pray to, or people who need scientific funding have to pray to. — BOOTS

33

# MY MURDER, MY LOVE

I recently got very into Michael Ondaatje and this is my version of a song that he might write, but it's really a breakup song. It's about the idea that your actions, not your thoughts, tell what your beliefs are. So it does pertain to a larger movement, but it's definitely about something in my life and it's maybe more trying to use some of the classical literary tools that some of my favorite writers might use.

It's not, I would say style-wise, it's not just Ondaatje, it's Salman Rushdie too. . . . I think I had just discovered him for myself so I read *Cinnamon Peeler, Coming through Slaughter*, and *The Collected Works of Billy the Kid*. Right now I'm reading *Divisadero*. But *The Cinnamon Peeler*, the collection of poems, that's my favorite by him.

I never believed poets. I just never believed it, it never could work for me. Maybe it's also because I also don't believe rappers. But with rappers I don't have to believe you, all I have to believe is that you have an ego and you want people to think you are good, because that's a lot of times what they are saying. So there's an honesty there.

# MY MURDER, MY LOVE

well, I've spoke the name of the lord in vain
in gunpowder and flame
and I've vomited slang in porcelain
and then claimed it was champagne
and i can rhyme silk with cigarettes
i can rhyme Jack Daniels with triumph
but no sentence i could spit could've shifted events
in the back of that Plymouth Reliant
and philosophy
is calculated to be worth its weight in air
but the way you told me to fuck myself
well, the words had a certain flair
i hope he fits the tux
i am just a man in flux
let me clarify things with the way I strut
so i can shout with my mouth shut

my murder, my love
what were the cookies made of?
my murder, my sweet
what kind of pill did we eat?

the machinery of lamps in the sky tonight
unfurl above electric lies of light
c'mon grip me tight against the wall
where the cusswords, piss, and masterpiece fight
i'm alive (through the power of explosion:
Colt 45 and a busted Trojan)
motion is evidence of belief
especially with the world's most beautiful slogan
applause from the mannequins should be ignored
look for the harmony of pen and sword
statues of our heroes turn to dust
we sing
to snort the dust up off the floor
i hope he fits the tux
even mountains are in flux
let us clarify things with the way we strut
so we can shout with our mouths shut

For a lot of my life I thought that poets were just more pretentious than even that. While I was reading them I could see them trying to impress me, but at the same time trying to seem like they're not trying to impress me, so I didn't like that.

Now there definitely have been fiction writers that I could say I believed, that I thought were just really trying to say something about life and trying to say something about the human experience in moments that existed and looking for ways to analyze that and looking for ways to record that and using language to expand on that. So there are writers like Toni Morrison, Gabriel García Márquez, people like that. But as far as the form of poetry, I think Pablo Neruda first opened me up to that, and then I read Michael Ondaatje and I really thought, I felt like he was writing for him. And I've definitely seen people writing for themselves and it didn't really impress me, I could see them doing that, but this was someone who was writing for himself that was trying to use other angles on thoughts, other angles on visually how you see a moment, that weren't just plays on words and it really made me appreciate him and how he was doing it in the form of poetry, you can't easily pick out the literary tool that he's using here and there and it just seems more like someone's immersed in it rather than using a trick. So that impresses me. — BOOTS

36

BOOTS RILEY

"2000, a flyer from one of the many organizations organizing against Prop 21." — BOOTS

OF UNITY

ND CULTURE TO DEFEAT
TH CRIMINALIZATION

grito serpentino

Latin rock, hip hop and spoken word

nt

p

street theatre

Local 1200 DJs

cists

OT THE ENEMY!

Februrary 26

Ballroom,

n St. (Oakland)

onations of $5-10 @ the door

th Promoting Advocacy And Leadership

510-869-6078/510-869-6033

"IT'S ABOUT THE IDEA THAT YOUR ACTIONS, NOT YOUR THOUGHTS, TELL WHAT YOUR BELIEFS ARE."

SORRY TO BOTHER YOU (2012)

# YOU ARE NOT A RIOT

## (AN RSVP FROM DAVID SIQUEIROS TO ANDY WARHOL)

For the last couple of albums, I have, a lot of times, been writing my lyrics in cafés. I'll go to San Francisco because although people might recognize me in both places, if I go to cafés in Oakland, folks in Oakland are people I might know from high school or whatever, and I don't feel necessarily OK with saying, "Hey, I'm working on something right now, I'll talk to you later," so I just don't get much done. So I'll go to someplace where I may not know people and I can kind of just go into my world and do it.

Somehow I overheard something in a café—I don't even remember what it was—I wrote this song five minutes after hearing it. But later I made it be about a fictional interaction between Andy Warhol (I've had a lot of debates with friends who, you know, are radical, who don't necessarily agree with this; whatever Warhol brought to the art world, he did put out there that he was

# YOU ARE NOT A RIOT
## (AN RSVP FROM DAVID SIQUEIROS TO ANDY WARHOL)

You, you are not a riot
You are right-wing terror military assault
You, you are not rebellion
You are a pretty piece of paper that is signed by murderers
You, you are not a riot
You are the tight leather pants on the old ex-general
You, you are not rebellion
I got the invite to your party and I threw it away

You, you are not a riot
You're an apologetic pad for the judge's gavel
You, you are not rebellion
You are a sitcom based on a torture chamber
You, you are not a riot
You are the fanfare for the king's drunken vomit
You, you are not rebellion
I got the invite to your party and I threw it away

A rebellion is both love and lust
and a riot is when lightning hits the right spot
and my painting isn't finished till it kills you
and it makes you feel more powerful than pills do

You, you are not a riot
You are a condo complete with wall-to-wall carpet bomb
You, you are not a riot
You're a well-funded beat-down in the boss's washroom
You, you are not a riot
You're the cold fish-breath of death at my neck
You, you are not a riot
I got the invite to your party and I threw it away

You fascist fashionista
You imperial chanteuse
You upper-crusty punk
You pillager's excuse
You Duke and Disciple of Disconnection
Who fellates the Empire State
Building blank space on your paper
Matching blank looks on your face

A rebellion is both love and lust
and a riot is when lightning hits the right spot
and my painting isn't finished till it kills you
and it makes you feel more powerful than pills do

You get hyped by the font in the death warrant
By the grain of the wood in the electric chair
The accent of the undertaker
By the architecture of police stations
By the reflection on the gun
By the crackle of the flame
You get hyped by the aesthetic of rebellion
No questions asked

You are not a riot

"Thousands marching on the Port of Oakland, California, in November 2011 in response to police brutality against Occupy.
— BOOTS

just doing what he was doing for money and seemed to be a very shallow person). And so you know, there are a lot of famous radical artists—one of the most famous muralists being Diego Rivera—but I wanted to get somebody crazy, and I was reading about David Siqueiros being at the Venice Biennale and accusing all these Latin American artists who were doing abstract art of being CIA agents. Which sounded pretty crazy I'm sure to a lot of people, and still sounds crazy, but the point that he was saying was that "Hey, we're in this time of revolution happening all over the world. You're one of the few people from your area that gets to talk to people all over the world, and what is it that you want to say? Nothing. So I think you're an agent."

Now we find out later that people like Jackson Pollack were getting funded through foundations that were funded by the FBI to make an apolitical art movement. So there may have been something to what he was saying. Siqueiros was a crazy dude, like a lot of actual revolutionaries end up being, and I don't agree with everything he did or said necessarily, but I think it was a great juxtaposition. What would somebody like Siqueiros say to Andy Warhol had he been invited to one of his parties?

—BOOTS

"SIQUEIROS WAS
A CRAZY DUDE, LIKE
A LOT OF ACTUAL
REVOLUTIONARIES
END UP BEING,
AND I DON'T AGREE
WITH EVERYTHING
HE DID OR SAID
NECESSARILY,
BUT I THINK
IT WAS
A GREAT
JUXTAPOSITION."

"This was an aerial view of merely part of one of two marches that went from downtown to the port during the Occupy Oakland general strike on November 2, 2011." —BOOTS

# LAND OF 7 BILLION DANCES

BOOTS RILEY

Insets: Stills from the video for "Land of 7 Billion Dances" by Yak Films.

# LAND OF 7 BILLION DANCES

Shake it
Yeah
We agitate it
Yeah
We bump and break it
Yeah
We finna take it
Hey now we gon'
Work it
Yeah
We jam the circuit
Yeah
We got the verdict
Yeah
It's fuck they circus

Electromagnetic with a bomb aesthetic
But we ain't breaded edit, got no credit
Listen real close to my phonetics:
The monster is awoke and I hope you fed it

If this your first time here, raise your hand
If the police come, hide the contraband
We all leave in a box and a long sedan
How you want your name read by the anchorman?

Drop the hips
Apocalypse
We ho'in out here cuz they got the chips
Like "Put it anywhere, but not the lips!"
Takeover
Let's plot the shit

Shake it
Yeah
We agitate it
Yeah
We bump and break it
Yeah
We finna take it

Hey now we gon'
Work it
Yeah
We jam the circuit
Yeah
We got the verdict
Yeah
It's fuck they circus

Shut 'em down—close the books
Them dudes in the boardroom—those is crooks
Take it to the street—bows and hooks
If you stop they money, they froze and shook

I'm a rap bandit—muthafucka, dabnabit!
And we been backhanded all across the Atlantic
And we finna start static all across the damn planet
Make they ass crap granite while we change the mathematics

I guess you all wonder why I called this meeting
Paycheck cut can't stop the bleeding
Sharks are feeding
We ain't eating
No more pleading
Time for stampeding

Shake it
Yeah
We agitate it
Yeah
We bump and break it
Yeah
We finna take it
Hey now we gon'
Work it
Yeah
We jam the circuit
Yeah
We got the verdict
Yeah
It's fuck they circus

# VIOLET

Stills from The Coup performing "Violet" in Chicago, Illinois, 2012.

"Violet" is another one we made the music for first. I think I came up with the idea of what the chorus would sound and feel like after we did the music and that kind of led me on an emotional journey. . . . I feel like there are a couple characters involved and in my mind it actually changes who I think the character is, but when I wrote it, Violet is a transgender prostitute who falls in love with somebody. I don't know who that is, but she's a prostitute and she's definitely struggling with a lot of things financially and is very depressed and falls in love with somebody who gives her hope for a small period of time and that person is not there anymore and that's it. That's the song. — BOOTS

## VIOLET

under hesitant flicker of neon glow
where the trash cans bloom and the needles grow
i wiped that shit off my mouth and i grabbed the dough
(and that's all y'all need to know)
let the glitter of the burning debris bless me tonight
is what I thought, and inhaled nicotine delight
screams for my life—scripted by deal memos
from the back of a bulletproof-steel limo
it ain't nothin in my life that's been real gentle
til the day of your magnificent beer swindle
told my story
you didn't look at me funny
and the kiss felt like you was payin me money

c'mon, holla at ya dog
c'mon, holla at ya dog
i must a missed yo call
c'mon

they said the sparkle in your eyes
was just cuz of the daggers
if they wanted us to leave they was gon have to drag us
skyscrapers crowded round to watch
as we laughed at the faulty perception of clocks
every 43 bus stop on Foothill could testify
your middle finger in the air was like blessin the sky
and the overpass
it shook like a overdose
and the rocks caught the holy ghost
and the wind made the chain-links sing falsetto
we made a promise we would never settle
standin on a hydrant
you declared it a holiday
against police and pimps we would have our way

c'mon, holla at ya dog
c'mon, holla at ya dog
i must a missed yo call
c'mon

the room and that dude had layers of filth
we sprinted out with the cash and got higher than stilts
i wondered if the birds were flyin to somethin
or flyin away
you said "both"
and hit the E & the J
now, the stars up there are for the few who use em
we karate'd down the block like the new solution:
street-level, eye-level, make your wish
you told me i could write a novel and make us rich
that's the last time i seen your crazy brown high-beams
I'm still in front of that buildin with the white screen
stop through for a hot second
holla back
i don't even want my fifty dollars back

c'mon, holla at ya dog
c'mon, holla at ya dog
i must a missed yo call
c'mon

# THIS YEAR

After I did the Tell Us the Truth tour with Tom Morello, Billy Bragg, and Steve Earle, I had seen Tom somewhere and asked him how the Audioslave record, which hadn't come out yet, was going. **And I asked him, "Is it going to be political? Is it going to be revolutionary? Who's writing?" And he was like, "Uh, yeah, I don't think it is. I've been trying to get him to go that way but I don't think it is." And he said, "Why don't you write a song that I can present to Chris? Write some lyrics and send them to me." So I wrote these lyrics, but they got turned down by Chris Cornell apparently. Anyway, so later on, Ry Cooder was producing Mavis Staples's album and we cut a demo of it with Silk E that was a much slower version. The story is I guess that Mavis really wanted to do it, but Cooder had different ideas for songs he wanted to put on there. It was for the album that ended up with the civil rights movement theme. So I was like, OK, the song has to come out, so we put it on this album. I think it's pretty self-explanatory what it is, hopefully it will become the new New Year's Eve anthem for people to have a revolution. Also, when I wrote it I thought about the New Year being the only holiday I can celebrate without any reservation. You know, there is May Day, but nobody here thinks of it as a holiday. It's something I can unite with everyone about—that time is moving on and there can be progression in your life, you can figure things out and move forward and that we all need to get drunk. So that's how "This Year" really fits.** — BOOTS

## THIS YEAR

This year will be the year
That we do what we've been waitin for
This year will be the year
That we stop knockin and kick down that door
Loved ones, we on the wire
Hesitation is the drug of choice
This time we're on fire
Make your mark on the world
Let em hear your voice

Cuz our life on this ball is just a blink of an eye
and ain't no fairy godmama gon' help you and I
Woke up this mornin
brushed my teeth and spit out the lies
Decided I'm gon live if I am gon have to die

And you can take it any way you want
You can take it any way you want
You can take it any way you want
You can take it any way you want
You can take it any way you want
You can take it any way you want
You can take it any way you want
But just take it

This time we get it in
We gon get em out they body, baby
This time we bust the ceiling
O-o-o-o-oh fa sho
We comin with tens of millions
Them villains be oh-so-shady
It's gonna be ending
With us winning
You already know

"We're sitting in a barbershop that obviously neither of us will use." — BOOTS

SORRY TO BOTHER YOU (2012)

WE'VE GOT A LOT TO TEACH YOU, CASSIUS GREEN

This is probably the song that is most directly related to the script that I wrote. Cassius Green is a character in the movie *Sorry to Bother You*. This is supposed to be a dream that he's having, but it also correlates with a point in the movie in which he's questioning one of his managers about how the world basically works. They're getting ready to train him to be one of them and they tell him, "We've got a lot to teach you, Cassius Green." The idea of the song is that the higher-ups believe in the way the world is working right now, and although we may know it's disgustingly unfair, there are a few who that think it's working the way it should be. They're trying to convince him of that.

In this story he's having a nightmare in which there are monsters, literal monsters, and he's in this high-rise office, afraid. And they're telling him that the world is the way it should be. They've got an assistant chained near them. There are creatures in the walls that are cheering along with everything that's going on. There are people downstairs howling from pain. He's looking at this whole situation and being told how all of this is the way it should be and decides that he doesn't want to be part of it, but then as he's leaving he realizes that actually he's a monster too and is part of it.

I think some of that has to do with the idea that we all think that we're not part of the system and it allows us to point the finger at everybody else. It allows us to not look at ourselves truthfully and it inhibits us from actually doing anything. It inhibits us from working with certain people or you know we just get an unrealistic view—even if we want to change things—of what it's going to take to change it. So he realizes that he's a part of the system.

—BOOTS

## WE'VE GOT A LOT TO TEACH YOU, CASSIUS GREEN

As the monster stood before his colleagues, he sang
angelically
and wiped the blood off his fangs
the papers on the boardroom table were stained
from corpses
piled on top of them slain
one monster yelled at me
"you've got the brains!"
and traced his claw along the table's woodgrain
it smelled like leather, Old Spice, and pain
his assistant, when yanked by choke-chain,
explained

We've got a lot to teach you, Cassius Green
We've got a lot to teach you, Cassius Green

The assistant crouched at the monster's feet
proudly
in a puddle of urine and meat
the monsters all howled at the morning spreadsheet
above cacophonous screams from below in the street
the gargoyles that guard the building weeped
I quietly calculated routes for retreat
one beast stuck his talons out as if to greet
and said "welcome to the good life, son. take a seat"

We've got a lot to teach you, Cassius Green
We've got a lot to teach you, Cassius Green

The beast who was frothing between his tusks
said "they work it, we run it. they shouldn't fuss.
the order of things is basically just"
I heard cheers from the creatures trapped in the air ducts
I told them to smother in their mountains of stuff
and headed to the elevator door in disgust
they said "you've forgotten. you're one of us"
I looked down at my tail, rattled it, and I cussed.

We've got a lot to teach you, Cassius Green
We've got a lot to teach you, Cassius Green
We've got a lot to teach you
We've got a lot to teach you
We've got a lot to teach you
We've got a lot to teach you

"In London, at Goldsmiths University, before a Coup show in 2012." — BOOTS

# LONG ISLAND ICED TEA, NEAT

Don't ever order a Long Island Iced Tea. If you are not familiar with what it is, it's just every alcohol that they can find poured into a glass with something sweet to maybe cut some of the taste and then there are some ice cubes. A Long Island Iced Tea, neat, is just more alcohol, because there are no ice cubes in there. I'd never order it, but I just—that was a long running joke between me and an ex-girlfriend, that we were going to order a Long Island Iced Tea, neat. There were a couple of bars that everyone would go to after some of the bigger early Occupy Oakland events, and there was a feeling of being in some historical moment and that, it wasn't a somber occasion, it wasn't all serious even though we knew that the moment was serious, people were becoming friends, making friends with each other. And there were a few bars around downtown Oakland that would get flooded after each one. I think that actually that led to people coming back. And actually that's how I ended up coming to Occupy Oakland a lot. My friend Andrej Grubacic was always like, "Oh, let's go get a drink at Radio." I can't

## LONG ISLAND ICED TEA, NEAT

I'll have a Long Island Iced Tea, neat
Or whatever kinda poison knocks me back in my seat
Cuz a little earlier we was out in that street
The police tried to smash and they felt defeat
You know they got no idea what they done unleashed
Keep my card open but it's done deceased
Them thiefs wanna talk when they cash decrease
Here's a toast to the folks who let action speak

I'll have a Long Island Iced Tea, straight
But the way my heart thumpin, I already levitate
Cuz a little earlier we made the whole earth quake
When we shut they shit down and had the boss irate
We only a fetus, we are modeling the shape
We gon make a masterpiece out of all the mistakes
But man I'm too damn drunk to continue this debate
Cuz I can't articulate and I need to urinate

I'll have one Long Island with one ice cube
Cuz as far as Rap go, he the muthafuckin dude
Let the record reflect that today we lit a fuse
(if I take one mo shot, I'm dancin on the bar nude)
Ay-Ay you talkin in my ear wit like hella amplitude
Every little fight could build up for the big feud
Today we struck a blow for all us in servitude
But the thousands of people got me drunker than the booze

Don't ever order a Long Island Iced Tea Neat.
Don't ever order a Long Island Iced Tea Neat.

Stills from interview with Davey D's Hip Hop
Corner–Davey D TV about Occupy Oakland.

SORRY TO BOTHER YOU (2012)

Boots Riley of the Coup
Unrest In Oakland over Police Attacking Occupy Oakland

Boots Riley of the Coup
Unrest In Oakland over Police Attacking Occupy Oakland

do his accent at all, it sounds Jamaican when I do it, but he's from Yugoslavia, and I'd say "OK" and we'd get out of the bar and he'd be like, "Well we've got to walk through Occupy Oakland," and I'd be like, "No, that's not on the way at all, we don't need to walk through Occupy Oakland." And so you know, I think he purposely tried to get me involved in that, and I'd meet people, and they'd ask me to come down or whatever and after a few of those times I eventually came down and got involved. Yeah, camaraderie was built there, even across the lines of all these factions—there were people I didn't know who were in different "factions" who were hanging out. Until later on when the lines were redrawn and focused on that I'd realize that people weren't in the same grouping or party. So yeah, I think that this song is one of the few songs that actually came from some of my experiences with Occupy Oakland. This also is a result of me hanging out with Japanther, this group from Brooklyn. We just went in the studio and the drumbeat is actually from this other Turf Talk song called "It's a Slumper," but just their interpretation of it, and Mike Reilly, no relation, wrote the line and it started—it felt jubilant in that way. **— BOOTS**

"This is a picture from one of the Occupy Oakland anti-foreclosure committee campaigns. They occupied a home that had been foreclosed and got the home back, and the loan renegotiated for the family."
—BOOTS

"THIS SONG IS ONE OF THE FEW SONGS THAT ACTUALLY CAME FROM SOME OF MY EXPERIENCES WITH OCCUPY OAKLAND."

# THE GUILLOTINE

Stills from the music video for "The Guillotine."

I think you can tell that I wrote it on an airplane, from the very first line, "We want to thank you for flying with us." "The Guillotine" is one of the songs I wrote after Occupy Oakland and this is probably the most Coup song on this album, in the sense that it's trying to be anthemic. The idea of the guillotine, it's not literal. It doesn't matter how many of the ruling class you kill; if you have the same system, then there will be more of them coming. It is about the power that the working class has to cut the head off the system, to get rid of the ruling class entirely by changing the system. But I could probably say that same explanation for a lot of my songs. This is a fun song to do live and it also is one of those with, in my mind, the feeling of Pink Floyd's "The Wall" in there. And it's funny because this song almost got cut from the album. We needed a different mix and we got that mix and it all of a sudden became good. There are a lot of songs that only end up being good songs when you listen to them from another angle, to figure out what they are about. — BOOTS

# THE GUILLOTINE

Hey, you

We got your war

We're at the gates

We're at your door

Hey, you

We got your war

We're at the gates

We're at your door

We got the guillotine

We got the guillotine, you better run

We got the guillotine

We got the guillotine, you better run

We got the guillotine

We got the guillotine, you better run

We got the guillotine

We got the guillotine, you better run

We wanna thank you for flyin with us

We know you coulda stayed home, just cried and cussed

May all your guns go off if it's time to bust

May all their tanks have time to rust

They got the armies turnin bullets into gold

They got the hookers turnin tricks in the cold

And everytime the police kicks in the do

An angel gas-brakes-dips in The 0

And even if a D-boy flips him a 0

It ain't enough to buy shit anymo

Sleep in the doorway, piss on the floor

Look in the sky wait for missiles to show

It's finna blow, cuz

They got the TV—we got the truth

They own the judges and we got the proof

We got hella people—they got helicopters

They got the bombs and we got the—we got the

We got the guillotine

We got the guillotine, you better run

We got the guillotine

We got the guillotine, you better run

We got the guillotine

We got the guillotine, you better run

We got the guillotine

We got the guillotine, you better run

Don't talk about, it's not a show

Be about it, it's bout to blow

Don't talk about, it's not a show

Be about it, it's bout to blow

I just spit the dope lines

I don't snort em

Tell the boss to call police to escort him

You don't write all them lies, you just quote em

Get offline, plug in to this modem

No you can't out-vote em

The rules are still golden

Only jewels we holdin

is if we guardin our scrotum

If you press your ear to the turf that is stolen

You can hear the sound of limitations explodin

Please, sir, may we have another portion?

We're children of the beast that dodged the abortion

Neck placed firm tween the floor and their florsheim

We'll shut your shit down—don't call it extortion

Caution—we're coming for your head

So call the feds and get files to shred

Every textbook read said bring you the bread

But guess what we got you instead

We got the guillotine

We got the guillotine, you better run

We got the guillotine

We got the guillotine, you better run

We got the guillotine

We got the guillotine, you better run

We got the guillotine

We got the guillotine, you better run

Let's keep it bangin like a shotgun

We're in a war before we fought one

Now if you're tired of workin so they can play—

A common enemy, we got one

Now keep it bangin like a shotgun

We're in a war before we fought one

Now if you're tired of workin so they can play—

A common enemy, we got one

Don't talk about, it's not a show

Be about it, it's bout to blow

Don't talk about, it's not a show

Be about it, it's bout to blow

WAVIP stands for "We're All VIP." Victor from Das Racist (which as of this writing is a group that doesn't exist anymore) used to be in a band with my cousin. **Now they're in a band again together. My cousin Loren was in a punk band called New Earth Creeps and another one called American Terrorists and Victor was the drummer for that and now they have a band together called Party Animal. So I've known Victor for a while and we were talking about doing a song together and at the same time talking to Killer Mike about doing a song. Killer Mike is actually good friends with my other cousin—usually everyone who's on our album is somehow involved in one way, shape, or form. I have a cousin named Dia Riley and she was the anchorwoman for ABC Atlanta for many, many years and now she's down in Florida somewhere, I think in Tallahassee. She's the anchorwoman there, and she was good friends with all the OutKast folks and so I knew Killer Mike in the nineties from that.**

**Because the term "99 percent" has been burned out, I definitely wanted to stay away from that. The only mention of 99 percent was in his verse, but the idea that we're all VIP I think I don't have to go into.... But yeah, he brings a real Ice Cube vibe to that, although the lyrics won't be printed because they're not my lyrics. I don't know if I've talked about it yet, but Ice Cube was a really big influence on me. It felt really good right there.**

**It's funny that "WAVIP" is the last song on my latest album to come out and it has that heavy kind of obvious Ice Cube influence in it. The first song that I ever wrote as The Coup is called "The Coup" and I think I took an Ice Cube song cadence and just put my own words into it. I forget which song, it might have been "Gangsta Gangsta,"**

"This was from the front line for the first march to the port during the general strike."
—BOOTS

## WAVIP

Chorus
We're All VIP
I'm talkin every muthafucka in my hood and me
I mean we're all VIP, VIP, VIP
We're All VIP
I'm talkin every muthafucka in my hood and me
I mean we're all VIP, VIP, VIP

You know I'm ballin soft
Make my drink a Molotov
Call it crunk or call it off
Swing it like a tomahawk
Middle finger at the cops
Rub us wrong—you get a spark
Bottle, pistol, or a rock
One day we gon call the shots
My flow it sputters like they shut off my water
I got the sheriff after me for what I said bout Obama
My flag is red like period—comma
I'm a piranha
just like every one ya'll—let's take that shark to the slaughter
Here we got a beat bouncin mo than last month's rent check
Boss walkin Wall Street with a pimp step
People of Whoville—we need to slit the Grinch neck
We low-paid prostitutes with no fishnets

We're All VIP
I'm talkin every muthafucka in my hood and me
I mean we're all VIP, VIP, VIP
We're All VIP
I'm talkin every muthafucka in my hood and me
I mean we're all VIP, VIP, VIP

so I might have been, "OK, he says it like this so I'm going to say it." I was nineteen or something like that. But definitely a lot of Ice Cube influence on everything. Not the song "Everythang," but on everything I do. I think he was one of the first who didn't have a New York accent and talked about things and situations that we thought were more "real." It wasn't "political." I think that everything is political. Ice Cube's lyrics weren't about world politics or US politics, but they were. It was talking about poverty and what people do to survive, and so I think a lot of people took it, felt a connection to it, and I think the problem with that whole movement of music at the time was that all these folks were wanting to talk about poverty and what it takes to survive, but there had been no movement to inform them, to give them an analysis of what it actually takes to survive, or what it takes so that people can do more than survive.

So people were saying things that they thought could be useful. You know when we started coming out with music, well-known rappers, who always get classified as gangster rap, would come up to us and say, "Yo, we're doing the same thing, I'm spitting that knowledge." They would write a song about how to cook crack cocaine because they thought that was giving some helpful knowledge to people. And the reason they thought that is only because the revolutionaries didn't get to them. So we would need to analyze how and why that didn't happen to talk about that movement. But getting back to Ice Cube, he was an idol of mine and when we started going to LA a lot to promote our first album, we would end up seeing Ice Cube in different places, and he would be friendly enough, saying, "Oh, how you doin'?" and come talk to us. But I was star-

"IT'S FUNNY THAT 'WAVIP' IS THE LAST SONG ON MY LATEST ALBUM TO COME OUT AND IT HAS THAT HEAVY KIND OF OBVIOUS ICE CUBE INFLUENCE IN IT."

struck and wouldn't say anything and not really know where to stand or sit. And I'm sure I made him feel really uncomfortable a lot of times, and it got to the point where I would go to his show and he would see me and be like, "That's Boots, I know he wants to come backstage; tell him to come backstage," and I'd be like, "No I didn't want that." And it was, you know, because I didn't want him to think I was a groupie or anything like that, which I was. After *Genocide and Juice* came out, I had this interaction with him. Ice Cube and OutKast were doing a show at the Warfield and I think I was back there and I was saying what's up to Cee Lo. Then Ice Cube saw me and said, "Hey Boots, come here, I've got to tell you something." And so I walked over to him and he was like, "Your music is very impressive, your work is very impressive." And then he turned his head as if he was looking to see who else was listening, "But let me tell you something. It's all about making that money." And then he walked away. So I don't know what, maybe he thought he was looking out for me. If you look at what he did during that time, he definitely was following his own advice. But so that was a strange interaction and it didn't necessarily feel good. But of course, I still hung on to him saying that my work was very impressive as being the highlight. I think that I definitely wouldn't mind being able to make money from what I am doing, but my reason for getting involved in the first place was something more than that. — BOOTS

# PICK A BIGGER WEAPON

# (2006)

1.  BULLETS AND LOVE
2.  WE ARE THE ONES
3.  LAUGH/LOVE/FUCK
4.  MY FAVORITE MUTINY
5.  I JUSTWANNALAYAROUNDALLDAYINBEDWITHYOU
6.  HEAD (OF STATE)
7.  SHOYOASS
8.  ASS-BREATH KILLERS
9.  GET THAT MONKEY OFF YOUR BACK
10. MINDFUCK
11. I LOVE BOOSTERS!
12. TIFFANY HALL
13. BABYLETSHAVEABABYBEFOREBUSHDO SOMETHIN'CRAZY
14. CAPTAIN STERLING'S LITTLE PROBLEM
15. THE STAND

# PICK A BIGGER WEAPON

Much of *Pick a Bigger Weapon* is about a relationship I was in. During the making of the album, my girlfriend and I were hanging out at a restaurant with that Detroit dynamo/poet Jessica Care Moore. My girlfriend liked to drink, and had thrown back five martinis. She was drinking with a purpose. When she ordered her sixth drink Jessica stopped her, saying, "Girl, pick a bigger weapon!" I said I was stealing that for the title of my album, which at that point was all about me falling in love with the woman at the table who couldn't feel her face anymore.

The first song I wrote for the album was "Laugh/Love/Fuck." I had just done the Tell Us the Truth tour with Billy Bragg, and this was me writing a song that Billy might have written if he rapped and liked Prince. The next song I finished writing much later was "Ijuswannalayaroundall-dayinbedwithyou." I told the label I was making headway on the album, and I was lying. Lying to them on the phone and lying in bed with my girlfriend, not getting things done. Andy Kaulkin, president of Anti/Epitaph, called me up one morning and asked if I had finished songs. I told him I had a lot of incomplete songs. Then I lied and said I had one finished song. He said, "Cool! I'm in Oakland today. I'll come by around 4." I had the music, but no lyrics. By 4 pm, I had the song, which was heavily inspired by the boss calling to check on my work. The title "BabyLet'sHaveA-BabyBeforeBushDoSomethin'Crazy" is a direct quote.

There are also a few in there that have no connection to my love life. "Tiffany Hall" is about a friend who died after having liposuction. The chorus and melody came to me a few seconds after I heard the news, and wouldn't get out of my head until I got some musicians in the studio and recorded it. — BOOTS

# BULLETS AND LOVE

"Bullets and Love," from *Pick a Bigger Weapon*, was actually the last song I recorded on that album. **Like "Everythang," it was a product of me listening to the album and realizing I needed something else.**

**We called musicians into the studio, I think they were Mike Auberge, Steve Weierman, and Elijah Baker maybe on bass.**

**I made a drumbeat, made the music, and I wrote those lyrics and, again, I probably put it all together in forty-five minutes. It wouldn't be on the album if I didn't like it. There are many songs that I might write in ten or twenty minutes, and because I'm not good at it, you'll never hear them. They're not good. The ones that you hear are the ones that I've done quickly and are on the album because they actually worked. — BOOTS**

## BULLETS AND LOVE

I'm
  a walkin contradiction
like
  bullets and love mixin'
  Slur my words
  with perfect diction
  I'm guilty
  of my convictions
  Complicated compositions
  punctuated propositions
  It's
  tenacious two-step
  audio
  with ambition
  Make you rev your transmission
  in the intersection
  twistin
  When the Henney hits the ground
  sidewalks will be christened
  I'm so nervous
  and sweaty
  that this gat might
  slip out my hand
  A homeless dude need a tip in his can
  He put his bid in this man
  now it's just bitterness man
  We need to bidness plan,
  I'm not just spittin at fans
  When I'm runnin from the police
  I don't have to rush

I'm so dope
I just jump
in the toilet and flush
We cut it
  boil it
  and hush,
  luminum foil it
  and such
  Tryin to catch
  the few bucks
  them big boys didn't clutch
  We use them tweezers for crutch
  when we done burned down the dutch
  But when they Starsky & Hutch
  We're just
  shit out of luck

# WE ARE THE ONES

"We Are the Ones" is a song that I started by first just writing the chorus to the music that I made and doing like what I heard somewhere. A chorus that felt somewhere in between Pink Floyd and Prince. Then, I wrote a story that is similar to other stories—a hustler talking about his transformation, the transformation in his worldview. In this case to see that we are the ones that have to change things.

The narrator of the story is a dope dealer and when I perform this on the recording and live, I do this really fake English accent, this posh English accent, "Once upon a time when crack was gold." This is going to be written so it doesn't matter—anyway, the reason for that was twofold. One, a great story writer, from before my recording time, is Slick Rick, and he has the English accent. Dana Dane also has an English accent and they both do a lot of

## WE ARE THE ONES

We
We are the ones
We'll seal your fate
Tear down your state
Go get yo' guns
We
We came to fight
It's yo' disgrace
Smash up your place
That's just polite
2x

Once upon a time
when crack was gold
And hip-hop was not yet platinum sold
I scoured the streets
for stacks to fold
My mood
like my hair
was relaxed and blowed
I hated police
and my teachers were beasts
My heat?
in the trunk of the classic Caprice
The one university I knew was Yale
So I cooked it
bagged it
put it on sale
Now philosophically
you'd be opposed
to one inhaling coke via mouth or the nose
But economically
I would propose
that you go eat a dick as employment had froze
And I felt like an abandoned child
Left to fend for myself in the wild
While every
Courtroom
judge and gavel
were there to bury me under the gravel

Or
at the bottom
of the finest malt ale
Observe
you'll find without fail
That in every neighborhood
and penitentiary
There exist many others who are similar to me
and

We
We are the ones
We'll seal your fate
Tear down your state
Go get yo' guns
We
We came to fight
It's yo' disgrace
Smash up your place
That's just polite

In later years
I lost some peers
Who mixed burners with Belvedere
And took shots
from gung-ho cashiers
The world was cold
yet
hell was near
So I saved for a kilo
And my stack got a little bit taller like Skee-Lo
A street CEO
There was all of this heroin and not one hero
The intensity was fortified
As I clenched five digits
on the forty-five
Belly down at the retail store
I would detail more
But I don't wish these actions to be glorified
If there was a plan
I was eager to listen
To not sleep in the park

PICK A BIGGER WEAPON (2006)

stories. But apart from that, I always thought it was interesting how, at least in the United States, someone with a posh English accent is thought to be more authoritative and people consider those folks experts on almost anything. So I thought that the protagonist in this story could benefit from the fake air of authenticity that's brought by that accent. Also I wanted to kind of tell the story in the same way that Masterpiece Theater might tell it.

That's where that comes from. And this is interesting, I often get asked about what it means when I say, "The one university that I knew was Yale, so I cooked it, bagged it, put it on sale." That's a play on the slang for cocaine, which is *yale*, and a lot of people thought because of the pronunciation through the '80s and '90s that the slang word was actually *yayo*, y-a-y-o, but how I came to know it was that yale, which was non–cracked up coke, the pure stuff, was called that because that's what the rich kids did. Cocaine was a rich kids' drug. I'm sure many folks know that. However, a lot of folks in the Black community never saw it that way.

Anyway, I have a lot of fun performing this, and I had a lot of fun writing this. This is one of those story raps that I do and kind of just is a thing that fits naturally with what I do. I went to film school and I really enjoy writing story raps. I don't want to fill my album with those, but it's always a good way to grab your listener and take them on your ride with you. I'm always looking for ways to do that. — BOOTS

"Because this is written so clearly, I'd guess that this is my studio copy of the lyrics, written over so I could understand my own writing." — BOOTS

WE ARE THE ONES VERSE 2

ER YEARS, I LOST SOME PEERS
ED BURNERS WITH BELVEDERE
SHOTS FROM GUNG-HO
LD WAS COLD, YET HELL WAS NEAR
NED FOR A KILO
STACK GOT A LITTLE
ET GE-0
AS ALL OF THIS

TENSITY WAS FORTIFIED
CLENCHED 5 DIGITS ON
OWN AT THE RETAIL STORE
LD DETAIL
DON'T WISH THESE ACTIONS

RE WAS A PLAN, I W
SLEEP IN THE PARK IN THE FETAL POSITION
TO WIPE OFF
NISE, I SURVIVE WITHOUT LEGAL PERMISSION

"I ALWAYS THOUGHT IT WAS INTERESTING HOW, AT LEAST IN THE UNITED STATES, SOMEONE WITH A POSH ENGLISH ACCENT IS THOUGHT TO BE MORE AUTHORITATIVE."

## WE ARE THE ONES
### {CONTINUED}

in the fetal position
Having to wipe off
canine fecal emission
Otherwise
I'd survive without legal permission
It's unequal division
and then we go to prison
which is a lethal decision
All I wanted
was the Regal to glisten
And my kids would have meat in the kitchen
I am complete ammunition
It's a given
once the people are driven
that

We
We are the ones
We'll seal your fate
Tear down your state
Go get yo' guns
We
We came to fight
It's yo' disgrace
Smash up your place
That's just polite

We like free speech
but we love free cable
We're taught from the cradle the Bill Gates fable
Which leads to high speeds
in Buick LeSables
We have no excuses
just great alibis
And poker faces
you cain't analyze
Our politicians sell our soul and our cries
With blood on their hands
they can't sanitize
We're the have-nots
but we're also the gon'-gets
Not just talkin 'bout the Lex with the chrome kits
(You can get that by yourself with a four-fifth)
Let's all own shit
then toast with Patrón hits

We
We are the ones
We'll seal your fate
Tear down your state
Go get yo' guns
We
We came to fight
It's yo' disgrace
Smash up your place
That's just polite

We are born from the mildew
the rust
the heathenous lust
The dreams in the dust
the evidence flushed
The grieving is just—
They're thieving from us
Insulted and cussed
This evening we bust
Our pay is unstable
and under the table

# LAUGH/LOVE/FUCK

I'm here to laugh, love, fuck and drink liquor
and help the damn revolution come quicker
Laugh, love, fuck and drink liquor
and help make a revolution
I'm here to laugh, love, fuck and drink liquor
and help the damn revolution come quicker
Laugh, love, fuck and drink liquor
and maybe make a revolution

Now this thing fin to end in fisticuffs
But if you gots to go 'head, twist it up
Unless your job finna make you piss in cups
Make you have to hustle rent with your pistols up
Now if Uncle Sam bomb us in his murder game
We gon' rise out the ash like that bird of flame
Hopin' you take action from the word I brang
But if the police ask, you never heard my name
Five years old
eyelids half-mast
Bedtime is 8 PM
it's half past
Try to take me to bed,
I'd make the mad dash
Scared in my sleep
I'd miss what had passed
Quarter century later, I'm still not sleepin'
If I'm not involved I feel I ain't breathin'
If I can't change the world, I ain't leavin'
Baby, that's the same reason you should call me this evenin'!

I'm here to laugh, love, fuck and drink liquor
and help the damn revolution come quicker
Laugh, love, fuck and drink liquor
and help make a revolution
I'm here to laugh, love, fuck and drink liquor
and help the damn revolution come quicker
Laugh, love, fuck and drink liquor
and maybe make a revolution

I'm finna take shots and make a mark
Not just take shots of Maker's Mark
That's how they make us marks
We got the drive to see the whole system break apart
We finna drive to the lake and park
Before we start
here's a club smelling like sweat, rum and perfume
She lettin' out whoops 'cause they playin' her tune
If we could, we would stay here 'til it were noon
Tell the sky we exist and resume
It's millennium three
We're collared and cuffed
It's a world conversation
I'm hollerin' stuff
Like we done wallowed in muck and
Squalor enough
Who's the culprit? Follow the buck
I'm just followin' up
'Cause like me
you gots to be in the middle of it
Unravellin' the riddle of it
And to do that you gon' ride on the powers that be
Well I'm finna ride with you
take me home in your little bucket

I'm here to laugh, love, fuck and drink liquor
and help the damn revolution come quicker
Laugh, love, fuck and drink liquor
and help make a revolution
I'm here to laugh, love, fuck and drink liquor
and help the damn revolution come quicker
Laugh, love, fuck and drink liquor
and maybe make a revolution

I'm not just jabber-jawsin'
We up against the wall
We can't just talk about it
Get all up in it y'all

## MY FAVORITE MUTINY

Death to the pigs
is my basic statement
I spit street stories
'til I taste the pavement
Tryin' to stay out the pen
where we face enslavement
Had a foolproof hustle
'til they traced the payments
I was grippin' my palm around some shitty rum
Tryin' to find psalm number 151
To forget what I'm owed
as I clutch the commode
I read put down the bottle and come get the gun
Let's get off the chain
like Kunta Kinte with a MAC-10
They want us gone
like a dollar in a crack den
Steadily subtractin' seeds and stems
Mind cloudy through the wheeze and phlegm
Numbin' my brain off of that
and the Jesus hymns
If we waitin' for the time to fight
these is thems
Tellin' us to relax while they ease it in
We gettin greased again
The truth I write is so cold
It'll freeze my pen
I'm Boots Riley
it's a pleasure to meet you
Never let they punk ass ever defeat you
They got us on the corner
wearin pleather and see thru

All y'all's goldmines
they wanna deplete you
I ain't just finna rap on a track
I'm finna clap on 'em back
And it's been stackin' to that
Five hundred years before
Iceberg ever leaned back in a 'lac
Before they told Rosa "Black in the back"
Before the CIA
told Ricky Ross to put crack in a sack
And Gil Scott tradin' rappin for smack
This beat alone should get platinum plaques
I'd rather see a million of us ecstatic to scrap
'Cause if we bappin' 'em back
we automatically stack

I ain't rockin' with you, so what what you goin do?
It's my favorite mutiny
I ain't rockin' with you, your logic does not compute
It's my favorite mutiny

# the coup

### oakland rapper brings powerful activist voice to the montreal international jazz festival

by brendan murphy, page seven

**PLUS INTERVIEWS**

with tortoise. béla fleck.
angélique kidjo. roy haynes.
eleni mandell. the besnard
lakes. chaka khan. bill frisell.
mr. scruff. nomo. derek trucks.
stefano bollani. cinematic
orchestra. allan holdsworth.
dawn tyler watson.
wayne krantz and more...

71

PICK A BIGGER WEAPON (2006)

## IJUSTWANNALAYAROUND
## ALLDAYINBEDWITHYOU

Monday rush

I'm s'posed to skip

But I just found Sunday

in yo' hips

Magic in the fingertips

and lips

Electric touch

Solar kiss

Thoughts wrangled up

legs tangled up

Baby do this feel good angled up?

Cain't be expressed by a single fuck

Wanna gently caress it and bang it up

And yo' smile

just seems so comfortable

Sho' wish

this clock wasn't functional

S'posed to be punctual

and not keep the boss waitin

But the sheet's sweatin

and the ceiling's pulsatin

Music from the birds and cars with beat

Stop pause repeat

the stars release

Y'know most of my time belongs to the boss

Baby hold on tight

this is ours at least


I just wanna lay around all day in bed with you

I just wanna lay around all day in bed with you

I just wanna lay around all day in bed with you

I just wanna lay around all day in bed with you

Givin head to you


Every sober mornin with you

is like we drunk at the Super 8

With laughin and plannin in between

while we recuperate

We communicate

with mouths fingers and hands

Cell phones with clocks

a-thousand-free-minute plans

Lose me in your details

break my codes

'Til all the good breakfast spots is closed

Them rich folks gots to knows

it's 'bout controllin these minutes

They can party

cause we work

'til our lower back goes

The world outside feels claustrophobic

Undercover of you

is where my thoughts exploded

Now

back to our ancient

lost aerobics

And the study of how bodies maybe tossed and folded


S'posed to get up for work

and ride on through

But last week he paid me with a IOU

I go to work at 9

if he don't pay me by 5

I'ma burn the place down by 5:02

Cause when we give 'em all of our ticks on the clock

They stack chips on the knot

we get pissed on a lot

We need a twist on the plot

but before we head to work

Scoot a little to the left

let me kiss on the spot


I just wanna lay around all day in bed with you

I just wanna lay around all day in bed with you

I just wanna lay around all day in bed with you

I just wanna lay around all day in bed with you

Givin head to you

# (HEAD) OF STATE

Bush and Hussein together in bed
Giving H-E-A-D
head
Y'all motherfuckers heard what we said
Billions made and millions dead
Bush and Hussein together in bed
Giving H-E-A-D
head
Y'all motherfuckers heard what we said
Billions made and millions dead

In a land not very far away from here
George W. Bush was drinkin beer
His daddy was head of the CIA
Now listen up close to what I say
The CIA worked for Standard Oil
And other companies to whom they're loyal
In a whole nother land by the name of Iran
The people got wise and took a stand
   to the oil companies
sayin "Ain't shit funny
This is our oil
our land
our money"
CIA got mad and sent false info
   to Iraq to help start the Iran/Iraq wo
Pronounced *war* if I have to be proper
The CIA is the cops that's why I hate the
   coppers
Saddam Hussein was their man out there
They told him to rule while keepin people
   scared
Sayin any opposition to him, he must crush it
He gassed the Kurds, they gave him his
   budget
Said "You gotta kick ass to protect our cash
Step out of line and feel our wrath"
You know the time without lookin at the
   little hand

Time came for them to cut out the middle
   man
Children maimed with no legs and shit
Cause the "Bombs Over . . ." you know
   the OutKast hit
And they really want you to hate him dead
When just the other day they made him head
War ain't about one land against the next
It's poor people dyin so the rich cash checks

Bush and Hussein together in bed
Giving H-E-A-D
head
Y'all motherfuckers heard what we said
Billions made and millions dead

Page image from *Montreal Hour*, vol. 15, no. 26, June 28–July 4, 2007.

THE COUP: HAS SOME QUESTIONS FOR
THE "UNDERGROUND"
photo: Alexander Warnow

picked up a microphone, he's a
...tion as much as words. Given
...latest album, *Pick a Bigger*
...like all their others, sets them
...rap's mainstream, we started by
...its relation to the underground.
...ink that's a false dichotomy that
...hen you say mainstream – you
...ally assume there is an under-
...hat is different," posits Riley.
...not, it's just a different style of
...d, unfortunately for the under-
...lot of the mainstream can rap
...und them."

...idea that mainstream rap is
...l and underground hip-hop is
...is pervasive. Boots, as he does
...mes during our conversation,
...cts this notion systematically.
...u have an industry that tells you:
...ke this kind of music, if you talk
...and if your video has this, you're
...t played on the radio. So when
...ve something more to say they'll
...t on their album somewhere, but
...s you see are much different... A
...groups that get criticized for talk-
...hustling and selling dope, at least
...king about some of the realities of
...and hustling to survive, while
...the groups that are considered
...l and underground, they just talk
...w much better of a rapper than
...re."

...ghing, he adds, "If you met
...y and they shook your hand and
..., I'm a really good guy' over and

...their upcoming Jazz Fest show,
...Pam the Funkstress) is being
...with a full funk band and singer
...hom he likens to a young Tina
...hich means that your ass will be
...s hard as your brain.
...back to the brain. When Boots
...a question, he answers the shit
...xample: I asked why, thematical-
...ms to frequently come back to
...economics, of capitalism versus

...anthropologist will tell you that cul-
...outgrowth of people figuring out
...vive and create. To survive under

that we talk about as if we don't know why
they're happening.

"There's been a whole bunch of
killings that happened this year in Oakland,
and someone else might say, 'All these
young black folks are going crazy,' either
because they have malice towards black
folks or because they refuse to look at the
fact that most of the people are getting
killed in some kind of dope thing, struggling for money. Why are they struggling for
money when we got all this money coming

coming into the Bay area and housing
prices are going up, the city is giving corporations tax kickbacks and not making
them hire people and prices are going up
for rent. So people are desperate.

"So yeah, I don't bring it back to capitalism, it gets brought back by itself."

PICK A BIGGER WEAPON (2006)

f, in re...lute roc
Besnard ...akes' ne
metrical ...pposite o
handiwork, ...will have
acteristics: ...ugh edge
esoteric pun...uation, a
while no on... – least o
placing betw...et, one
The grand, ...xtured s
record has ...e poise, i
tus of a once-in-a-lifeti...

"We were definit...
record had to be the ...
possibly make," says b...
writer Olga Goreas. "...
put as much of ourselv...
– and we did. I guess it...
of situation."

The way Gore...
singer/songwriter Jace ...
at it, it had been a go...
their first formal outi...
there was "like, no way...
out another record in...
with the Montreal b...
enough to ease the p...
seemed riper than ever...

And so, with a litt...
tears, a lot of intuition, ...
that could lend a "soli...
to the record (the oth...
White, Steve Raegele, ...
Kevin Laing), and a ...
resources needed to ...

THE COUP

At Club Soda (1225 St-Laurent),

# SHOYOASS

Now's the time for you to show yo ass
They ain't handin out no mo cash
Mommas imitate my logo fast
Daddies take the safety off and blast
Now's the time for you to show yo ass
They ain't handin out no mo cash
Mommas imitate my logo fast
Daddies take the safety off and blast

Now this is mo' mean than four fiends with glocks
unloading
Scrappin for a bag of gold rings and codeine
Whole life savings hid under the molding
Mama said "Knock Them Out" and I'm quoting
You're voting
which you're hoping
will stop the guns from smoking
is someone fucking joking?
They're bankers in sheep's clothing
I know places where the kids keep croaking
Lacking the essential vitamins and protein
Hustlin and hyphy are eloping
I'm the best man bustin shots and toasting
Sippin Grey Goose
get clipped off the bird
Come Sunday mornin
get tripped off the word
TV and them preachers got pimp talkin verbs
Settin us up to get ripped off and stirred
You flipped all them birds so your funds act right
Here come the drought
whole thangs half price
My high school career counselor's advice
"Little niggers: act nice for your beans and rice"
I got some light baby, take it to the head
I gives a fuck if it's permed or in dreads
Never snitch to the locals or the feds
See they tryna break us
so they don't have to break bread
Cause Uncle Sam ain't the baker
he's the butcher
We all on Punk'd with no Ashton Kutcher

Where ballin (not broke) cutthroats kaput ya
Ain't never took dope but them dopes done took ya
Stop flyin Ol' Glory man
cut it down
If your job ain't payin right
shut it down
If your car got 18's
let it pound
and if we ever gon do it
let's do it now

Now's the time for you to show yo ass
They ain't handin out no mo cash
Mommas imitate my logo fast
Daddies take the safety off and blast
Now's the time for you to show yo ass
They ain't handin out no mo cash
Mommas imitate my logo fast
Daddies take the safety off and blast

You're in a system where they
flirt with disaster
Tongue kiss death
have mass murder orgies
til there's no one left
They're finger-fuckin Lady Liberty under her dress
And since I didn't say this under my breath
I might be under arrest
now lemme introduce
My slave name's Ray Riley
you can call me Boots
Cause we gon' boot 'em outta power
then spread the loot
We need to drive that freedom train
not ride caboose
And you can tell by the way I walk my walk
That there's a coroner behind me
holdin chalk
Cause he works for the county
who works for the state
Who works for the boss man
eatin off your plate
We ain't one dimensional, max-detentional
Lookin for the liquor store

"What them hubbas hittin fo'?"
We're raised by the street light
praised for the street fight
Days we ain't eat right
hazed to complete life
Had to make homes outta muck
and dirt
Just to get dinner take luck and
work
They don't need my rights, they
induct a curse
So you're cordially invited to go
buck berzerk

Now's the time for you to show
yo ass
They ain't handin out no mo cash
Mommas imitate my logo fast
Daddies take the safety off and
blast
[2x]

The black is heated; baby, yeah
A hundred Fahrenheit
Act a fool, show yo' ass
Let's make it alright
2x

It's introduction of a new breed
of leaders
Stand up organize
It's introduction of a new breed
of leaders
Stand up organize
It's introduction of a new breed
of leaders
Stand up organize
It's introduction of a new breed
of leaders
Stand up organize

The block is heated
baby yeah
A hundred Fahrenheit

Act a fool
show yo' ass
Let's make it alright

## ASS-BREATH KILLERS

Some confuse ass-breath with strong halitosis
It's been hundreds of years since the first diagnosis
By the African doctor Mawangi Misoi
Known in the states as Mr. Thomas's boy
He found that preventing this affliction was lost
with the mention of the phrase, "Um, yassuh, boss!"
When that phrase was uttered many stomachs would wrench
Some jumped in the Atlantic to escape the stench
He noted ass-breath came from kissin ass a lot
To be the boss's knight-in-armor like Lancelot
Doctor Misoi years later (before he was hanged)
Developed pills with the taste of lemon meringue
Made from ground gunpowder of Haitian slaves
And sweat from Seminoles who just wouldn't behave
He tested first on young Nat from the Turner plantation
Then sent a batch off to the French speakin nation
It should also be noted, a bottle of it was found
in the clenched dead hand of the white John Brown
Everytime it went round, new people refined it
They would take their essence, put it in and grind it
In Russia, Africa, Asia too
Mao Tse-Tung made the flavors new
In Cuba, the people make new shipments
of this pill that is on the FDA shit-list
They say it's not recommended, to take before dinner
With supervisors, presidents, or such type sinners
Take this pill and say what you wish you said
It hardens backbones, they might wish you dead
And it's not to be confused with courage juice
Which we drank in chains and we still ain't loose
These pills really should be taken in groups
Cause ass-breath muthafuckas move with troops
MLK took half a pill, procrastinated
Once he took a whole pill, they assassinated
Take Ass-Breath Killers, to really get down
Wherever rocks, fire, and struggle are found

When it's time to speak up and you can't make a sound
Take the pills that'll make you kick the king in his crown
Take Ass-Breath Killers, to really get down
Wherever rocks, fire, and struggle are found

ASS BREATH BRAIN

REBELLIONS

NAT TURNER — SOUTHAMPTON VIRGINIA
TOUSSANT L'OUVERTURE
~~SI~~ CINQUE ~~DESSALINES~~ HAITI
AMISTAD

FRENCH REVOLUTION
RUSSIA
CHINA
CUBA
VIETNAM

From live video of "Ass-Breath Killers," shot by Vince Tocce.

## GET THAT MONKEY OFF YOUR BACK

Chorus
Get that monkey off your back
Get that monkey off your back
Get that monkey
Get that monkey
Get that monkey off your back
Get that monkey off your back
Get that monkey off your back
Get that monkey
Get that monkey
Get that monkey off your back
Get that monkey off your back boy
Get that monkey off your back girl
Get that monkey off your back
Get that monkey off your back boy
Get that monkey off your back girl
Get that monkey off your back

You know it ain't for us
You know they think we dangerous
Even with no thangs to bust
They wanna keep puttin chains to us
That's why I constantly sang and cuss
And when I bring it it's a gang of fuss
They tryin to send us out to bang for bucks
They must be off of that angeldust
so check it out

Chorus

I'm an instigator
Mashin out or in the scraper
And you can listen at me now or later
But stop givin them pimps your paper
Used to be caught up in them capers
Havin to hustle, rustle up my status
They beat my yellow ass purple like the Lakers
More like the Clippers cause they tryin to fade us
now holla wit me

Chorus

Aight we finally gots new momentum
Let's fill the fridge up in the kitchen
It's lotsa pots for cookin D-boy chicken
But we still ain't gots one to piss in
They say I'm always fittin the description
Of selling unprescribed prescriptions
But it's them with the green addiction
Think we gon' have to shake 'em off and keep dippin
so sing along

Chorus

BOOTS RILEY

"From a discussion with M-1 of Dead Prez in Santa Cruz." —BOOTS

# MINDFUCK

Mindfuck
they don't have to put our hands
   in cuffs
They can tell us stay put
and that's enough
We bust
they feel the earth vibratin
It ain't a earthquake
we just need a new equation


The fog pours in like the thickest cream
Nightfall comes and the crickets scream
Deafened by the latest lotto ticket
schemes
Cement lies and white picket dreams


The pain on his face is glistening
No one's eyes are listening
'Til his 44 starts whistling
Hairs on necks—
Bristling


You can holla so loud 'til the silence
comes
Ask that hustler with the Midas tongue
He was born after you but not quite
   as young
Waitin for the day when the fighters
   come


She said, "Seem like traffic lights is
   always red"
"Your application's on file," is all they
   said
She wish the great leaders wasn't
   always dead
She could resurrect 'em inside of her
   instead

Mindfuck
they don't have to put our hands in
   cuffs
They can tell us stay put
and that's enough
We bust
they feel the earth vibratin
It ain't a earthquake
we just need a new equation


He was killed in the end by quiet
   persuasion
Not the FBI home invasion
Nor the cross on his lawn emblazoned
The predictable fights didn't faze him
Bullhorns off
Holidays given
House notes
nine to five prison
He yells at the news
sayin, "There'd be a movement
if the new generation was a little more
   driven"


One mind
two hands
four walls
She says Babylon's gon' fall
She'll tell you the signs
since everybody's dumb
She'll be home waitin for the Messiah's
   phone call


There was pride in the fact that the
   blunt was massive
Tight like the ships in the middle
   passage
They escaped through the flames, then
   wondered
If the flame in their soul, if the smoke
   had smashed it

Mindfuck
they don't have to put our hands in
   cuffs
They can tell us stay put
and that's enough
We bust
they feel the earth vibratin
It ain't a earthquake
we just need a new equation


Day breaks in like a fiend with a ladder
Suicidal dew drops splatter
Teeth on shirtless bodies chatter
A blowjob short of a breakfast platter


Crowded rooms on lonely souls
At work before the whistle blows
They never knew their strength in
   numbers
So power seems so mystical
They're waiting for that perfect day
When they've paid all their bills
They kids are grown
they graduate
And guerillas come out the hills


And for her it gets too much
'Til she won't accept my touch
She'll fix it by herself
She's fallen into their mindfuck


They're givin us a mindfuck
They don't have to put our hands in
   cuffs
They can tell us stay put
and that's enough
We bust
they feel the earth vibratin
It ain't a earthquake
we just need a new equation

# I LOVE BOOSTERS!

I love them boosters
They love them boosters
You should love em too
Even if they don't know ya
They'll get it for ya
Like a whole outfit or shoe

A booster is a person
who jacks from the retail
And sells it in the hood
for dirt cheap resale
In these hard times
they press on like Lee Nails
In all of my experience
their sex has been female
Back in elementary
my shoes used to rap
Every time my soles hit the street
they would flap
Then in high school
Langston Anderson would cap
'Cause my jacket didn't have
a brand name on the back
Years later
this lady took me to her apartment
It looked like the Macy's sportswear
    department
Clothes on the chairs
on the couch
and the carpet
A twenty had me icy
like pissin in the Arctic
If it wasn't for the hard work
of a booster
Most couldn't go to the clubs
that we're used to
If you don't fit the dress code
they'll boot ya
Like people who get dressed up
won't shoot ya
For some of y'all folks
this stuff might faze ya

This ain't the way
that society raised ya
But most of it
was made by children in Asia
The stores make money
off of very low wages
The next time you see two women running
out the Gap
With arms full of clothes still strapped
    to the rack
Once they jump in the car
hit the gas
and scat
If you have to say something
just stand
and clap

I love them boosters
They love them boosters
You should love em too
Even if they don't know ya
They'll get it for ya
Like a whole outfit or shoe

This goes out
to all them hard-working women
Who risk jail time
just to make them a living
We know there'd probably be
no one in prison
If rights
to food, clothes, and shelter
were given
Plus
they be keepin me
dressed so fresh
Even when my wallet
yells S.O.S.
In a cheaper Sunday suit
you feel a little more blessed
So until the revolution that I profess
My shirt is from Stacey
my pants are from Rhonda
My shoes came out the trunk

of a baby blue Honda
My wardrobe's in luck
if something falls off a truck
If you're looking for some leather
then go see Yolanda
If I'm on the red carpet
and they ask who designed this
I'mma give a shout-out
to Bay Area's finest
All on our own
we survive this with slyness
But when we come together
all our fashion is flyness

I love them boosters
They love them boosters
You should love em too
Even if they don't know ya
They'll get it for ya
Like a whole outfit or shoe

TIFFANY HALL

Tiffany Hall
It appears we didn't know you at all
Hey hey hey hey hey
With this song I write your name on the wall
Tiffany Hall
It appears we didn't know you at all
Hey hey hey hey hey
With this song I write your name on the wall
Tiffany Hall

You was all smiles and no games
Teeth white as cocaine
Dark skin, knew about the struggle and the dope game
Quick to spark a convo into flames like propane
Filled the air, and I was thrilled you cared
In summer bridge hiding from the tutors
Bumpin gums about the future
You claimed that one day we'd be ruled by computers
I said, "It's like that now cause we all machines"
And you replied, "But I'm a robot with dreams"
Which I thought was clean
And all the fellas used to talk about ya
How you had a joyful aura and a walk about ya
Necessitated by a beautiful backside
We thought you was fine
And we didn't let the facts hide
Nevertheless we would call you "waddle waddle"
Somebody shoulda slapped us with an old hot water bottle
Could called you "talky talky" or nothing at all
I was crushed when I got the call

Tiffany Hall
It appears we didn't know you at all
Hey hey hey hey hey
With this song I write your name on the wall
Tiffany Hall
It appears we didn't know you at all
Hey hey hey hey hey
With this song I write your name on the wall
Tiffany Hall

You had warmth and sincerity, a heart with no barriers
A laugh that made slightly funny turn hilarious
While everybody else mouthed off about answers
You got up and started workin with some ex–Black Panthers

Leadin campaigns and writin in they newspaper
You always seemed happy
an idea that I would lose later
We would see each other sayin "Stay in touch"
But I was just like you
always busy
in a rush
Told yo' mama I was writin this
she said it was blessin
I'm just chantin your name out loud
and confessin
That maybe I was part of your demise
You went and got liposuction on your ass and thighs
Came straight home as you slept that evenin
Bloodclots from the operation stopped you from breathin
Your shape was great if I may say so
way before J-Lo
Whoever told you it wasn't had horns not a halo
Or is it just that your behind was up to discuss?
Cause as a man
mine ain't talked about much
Dear Tiff
I wish the world wasn't missin yo vision
Sincerely
one mo' robot with a dream and a mission

Tiffany Hall
It appears we didn't know you at all
Hey hey hey hey hey
With this song I write your name on the wall
Tiffany Hall
It appears we didn't know you at all
Hey hey hey hey hey
With this song I write your name on the wall
Tiffany Hall

Hey Tiffany! We love you! (8x)

## BABYLET'SHAVEABABYBEFOREBUSH
## DOSOMETHIN'CRAZY

Baby let's have a baby before Bush do somethin crazy

Baby let's have a baby before Bush do somethin crazy

I don't want the world to blow

before we get a chance to let our love grow

I don't want the world to blow

before we get a chance to let our love grow


I don't really wanna fuss and fight

Baby we might have numbered nights

We might never get our money right

We could take off this patch tonight

Bombs goin off everywhere

The police got us runnin scared

But I still got some love to share

Plus you know I stopped smokin squares

# CAPTAIN STERLING'S LITTLE PROBLEM

BOOTS RILEY

Stills from video by Vince Tocce of The Coup performing live at Mezzanine in San Francisco, Fall 2005.

CAPTAIN STERLING'S LITTLE PROBLEM

Get yo' ass off the flo' (5x)

It's a wrap then
Grab the MAC-10
Plan of action
Kill the Captain
Excuse me colonel sir
May I request please
Permission to go home
Or blow off your knees

It's a wrap then
Grab the Mac-10
Plan of action
Kill the Captain
In case you're wonderin
Well, yes, I'm gon' fight
I'm finna join the army
But one you don't like

Needed some stackoli to get free like a parolee
Now I'm in apparel colored shit and guacamole
In another country brought to you by Coca-Coley
Ordered from the top to shoot everything holey
Shit I'm 19 and I'm missin all my homies
All that fight for freedom shit

we know that shit is phoney
Free to work at Shoney's
bout one hour for six boneys
And every day we hustle scratch and scrape for macaronis
and cheese
bullets squeeze outta my assault weapon
Tear through the air
then his chest
then his breaths end
Looked like my homie from the hood I be reppin
I wept then
changing from a soldier to a veteran
Left in shambles
bout this kin of no relation
Crept in the sergeant's tent with quiet calculation
Message from the soldiers
to the brass administration
Looks like Captain Sterling's finna have a situation
It's a wrap then
Grab the MAC-10
Plan of action
Kill the Captain
Excuse me colonel sir
May I request please
Permission to go home
Or blow off your knees

It's a wrap then
Grab the Mac-10
Plan of action
Kill the Captain
In case you're wonderin
Well, yes, I'm gon' fight
I'm finna join the army
But one you don't like
Get yo' ass off the flo' (4x)

"I have just killed my first but it may not be the last one"
I screamed this at the sergeant
with his head press to the magnum
You brought us to this country
not to free

but bodybag
them
And free up all their money so accounting firms can add them
Drag them
and their corporates
to their own battle
Now they're dragging us to the slaughter like cattle
Me and this whole unit we will start to ramshackle
Listen very closely you can hear the fire crackle
You could weigh the air
as he was breathing out his nostrils
Couldn't understand why we were seeming so hostile
Said "We spread democracy" like he was preaching gospel
Slapped him in his head and said "Now shut up Sergeant Roscoe!
If this is not explicit
lemme tell ya straight out
We'll no longer kill
to keep this country drained out
We want up outta here
like on the next planes out
Tell the Cap'n make it happen or we'll blow his brains out!"

It's a wrap then
Grab the MAC-10
Plan of action
Kill the Captain
Excuse me colonel sir
May I request please
Permission to go home
Or blow off your knees

It's a wrap then
Grab the Mac-10
Plan of action
Kill the Captain
In case you're wonderin
Well, yes, I'm gon' fight
I'm finna join the army
But one you don't like

Get yo' ass off the flo' (4x)

# THE STAND

THE STAND

This is the place where I take my stand
Take my stick and draw a line in the sand
Show my hand
Initiate the actions planned
Now meet the rubber on my shoe or meet my fuckin
demands
Here's the place where I take my stand
Take my stick and draw a line in the sand
Show my hand
Initiate the actions planned
Now gimme time for assault or gimme back my clams

As saltwater drips from my oculars
I got the urge to just squeeze on the glock and burst
My fingertips wipe away my teardrops
I curse
You diggin in my purse
so may you rock a hearse
This feeling's popular cause people's kids need socks and
shirts
And if you po' you get wopped the worst
Hopes of Hollywood endings
without plot the first

Be happy all I did so far is drop a verse
See I'm old school like coke lines and LP covers
Learned how to hustle then run when the heat hovers
Fist to my heart,
warm embrace:
how I greet others
Cookin with no lights makes my fish burn like Deep Cover
Keep cover
cause I'm finsta spray
I go from sun up to sun down and miss the day
You been sayin for months
that you gon' fix my pay
While the hours of my life get pissed away

This is the place where I take my stand
Take my stick and draw a line in the sand
Show my hand
Initiate the actions planned
Now meet the rubber on my shoe or meet my fuckin demands
Here's the place where I take my stand
Take my stick and draw a line in the sand
Show my hand
Initiate the actions planned
Now gimme time for assault or gimme back my clams

Weed and dope
Speed and hope
When we bleedin broke
we get keyed and cope
When ecstasy pills don't stop SBC bills
We get all depressed
like we need a rope
Poundin walls
cain't handle it
Ten days with the candles lit
When the fridge cheese is green
and the pocket cheese is silver
Ain't no hustle too scandalous
And I'm a champion
at runnin my mouth
But I'll be campin
if I'm kicked out the house

So here's my anthem
sing it to the music or shout
I forfeit the rat race to start the 12 round bout
I got your damn IOU in my hand
Thankin of things I can do with two grand
But I'ma light it with a Bic
then use it as a wick
To burn your shit down cause I'm through with you man
Less you pay me

This is the place where I take my stand
Take my stick and draw a line in the sand
Show my hand
Initiate the actions planned
Now meet the rubber on my shoe or meet my fuckin demands
Here's the place where I take my stand
Take my stick and draw a line in the sand
Show my hand
Initiate the actions planned
Now gimme time for assault or gimme back my clams

Mama
never raised no punks
no
Brawlin but not crawlin
Time to put my all in
Mama
never raised no punks
no
Brawlin but not crawlin
We starvin but y'all ballin

PICK A BIGGER WEAPON (2006)

# PARTY MUSIC (2001)

1.  EVERYTHANG
2.  5 MILLION WAYS TO KILL A CEO
3.  WEAR CLEAN DRAWS
4.  GHETTO MANIFESTO
5.  GET UP
6.  RIDE THE FENCE
7.  NOWALATERS
8.  PORK AND BEEF
9.  HEVEN TONITE
10. THOUGHT ABOUT IT 2
11. LAZYMUTHAFUCKA

# EVERYTHANG

"Everythang" is a song with a lot of generalizations, obviously. Many of them are true—generalizing yet being a correct definition of what's going on, so for instance, "Every cop is a corrupt one, if you ain't got no cash up in the trust fund." It's basically just saying that if police are arresting you for crimes that you do that are petty, yet they don't arrest the rich for crimes that they do, which are further reaching and affect more people, then that cop, that whole police system is corrupt, and that cop is corrupt for being part of it.

There are other ones that are not true. "Every cat with a gat wanna bust one." No. Feels like that sometimes, but no, everybody with a gun does not want to shoot it. But the whole idea is that there are a lot of blanket statements being put to give the feeling of absolute truth, of absolute certainty and each verse ends with "Every broke

"EVERY-
THING
THAT
YOUR EYE
CAN SEE,
EVERY-
THING
THAT IS
NATURAL,
EVERY-
THING
AROUND
YOU IS
SOME-
THING TO
SHARE."

muthafucka finna form a gang and when we come we takin' everythang."

You know, to end with that idea, that everything belongs to the people. So it kind of goes along with that whole idea, of sharing and the idea of everythang. Everything that your eye can see, everything that is natural, everything around you is something to share. Now obviously, the details of how that would happen in a communist system, that could be debated forever—will people have their own this or that? Yes, they will. But the point is that the resources are not for hoarding.

Also back to the beginning idea that "every cop is a corrupt one, if you ain't got no cash up in the trust fund." I refer to that later when I say, "Every crime that I did was petty, every criminal is rich already."

That was our electronic take on Fela [Kuti]'s *ITT* (*International Thief Thief*). It's a lot different. It's not Fela's *ITT*, but we were going off of that feeling and that mood.

This is always a fun one to perform. — BOOTS

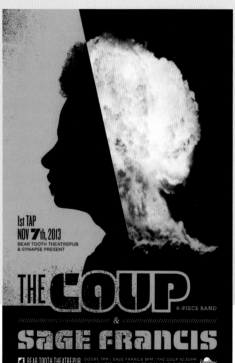

From the poster for a 2013 show in Anchorage, Alaska.

# EVERYTHANG

everybody throw your lighters up
tell me
y'all finna fight or what?
everybody get your shit started
this is y'all motherfuckin party
everybody throw your lighters up
tell me
y'all finna fight or what?
everybody get your shit started
this is y'all motherfuckin party

Every death is an abrupt one
Every cop is a corrupt one
If no cash up in the trust fund
Every cat wit a gat wanna bust one
Every guest want a plus-one
Every tenement's a penitent
So every tried man is innocent
Time served should be the sentence spent
Everybody wanna hit a lick
Every one a y'all is getting pimped
Every time I spit I'm finna rip
Every cancer is a homicide
Every boss better run and hide
Every human is some kin to Black
Every Visa got a pin to crack
Every verse is from the cardiac
Every search is involuntary
Every inmate want commisary
Every bank note is promissory
Every broke muthafucka finna form a gang
and when we come
we takin everythang

everybody throw your lighters up
tell me
y'all finna fight or what?
everybody get your shit started

this is y'all motherfuckin party
everybody throw your lighters up
tell me
y'all finna fight or what?
everybody get your shit started
everybody get your shit started
this is y'all motherfuckin party

Every mack want a Cadillac
Every mark want they scrilla back
Every knock want a hit of crack
In the park or a Pontiac
Every little cent is to the rent
And every roach is a resident
Every truth ain't evident
Every slave story, present tense
Every uprise a consequence
Every time it be something sweet
Every banker is a fuckin thief
Everybody betta holla wit me
Every fiend need a dolla fifty
Every crime that I did was petty
Every criminal is rich already
Every landlord got a complex
Every single is a bomb threat
Every sellout mayor hates my verse
Everybody, they gon' get it first
Every broke muthafucka finna form a gang
and when we come
we taking everythang

everybody throw your lighters up
tell me
y'all finna fight or what?
everybody get your shit started
this is y'all motherfuckin party
everybody throw your lighters up
tell me
y'all finna fight or what?
everybody get your shit started
this is y'all motherfuckin party

# 5 MILLION WAYS TO KILL A CEO

The title for some is an obvious shoutout to a dance hall song where they say "five million ways to die, choose one," which I think that might actually come from a movie or something. I had recorded the music in the studio already and was just kind of listening to it and somehow the title came to me.

I think Public Enemy did a song a few years before called "How to Kill a Record Executive," or something like that. But this one I wanted to purposely, one, be danceable—the music was already done, so there. But also, the writing of it, the style of it, was dictated a little bit by the beat, which is a really weird beat. It's danceable because we made the beat four on the floor. But it's like, the count is something like 9/17 or something weird like that. So it's not a four on the floor thing. I wanted to make it danceable, but I shot myself in the foot by doing a weird count like that because a lot of DJs that want to play it, they're like "we can't figure out a way to mix it in right."

So anyway, I think on this album, on *Party Music*, I really started thinking, at least more than I had been, about making beats that DJs could play. I think "Everything," was definitely conceived of more in that vein—that DJs would play at a party.

So, I wanted to make this comical. I already knew that the last verse would be the comical conclusion that it was, you know. It's funny because—many times by my detractors—I get called a little too heavy, or my work gets called dogmatic. But actually, most of my lyrics are pretty tongue in cheek. I would probably not make a song about literally killing a CEO. Not because I have a problem with it per se, but because that wouldn't be a fun song. The things that I think motivate people into action are not doom and gloom, and not anger and rage, the things that I think actually motivate people into action are optimism and hope.

So when I do talk about things like this and the terrible things that the ruling class has done, I talk about it with the optimism and hope of changing it. And when I try to draw class lines in my songs, I do so with humor, with showing the irony that exists in the world.

Often people see the title, "5 Million Ways to Kill a CEO," and they picture a vicious attack on the system. I don't know, it's up to you to say whether this is a vicious attack on the system. I clearly do not like the system of capitalism, and to make it clear, would like there to be a world in which the people democratically control the profits that they create, and that would be communism, socialism, whatever you want to call it. But "5 Million Ways to Kill a CEO," if you look at the last verse, I list the

5 million ways to kill a CEO, and it's basically them being killed by their own greed.

Anyway, I don't really like listening to songs about doom and gloom. Whether they're about a relationship or about the system. Even songs with sadness I want them to have some optimism in them, and if I'm going to make a song with my view on the world, since I'm very optimistic about the people's ability to change the world, that optimism is going to show up in my music and in my lyrics.

There is a lyric at the beginning of the second verse that says, "Suck this game in slow, it's the creeper. If you is the janitor get a street sweeper," that is the lyric that caused us to name the band that I have with Tom Morello "Street Sweeper Social Club." A street sweeper is an automatic shotgun, a machine gun that shoots shotgun shells. It's a very, very savage weapon that actually was first sold en masse to South African police in the 80s.

Anyway, we called ourselves the Street Sweeper Social Club because our music is a weapon—that's been said before. We said it in a different way. —BOOTS

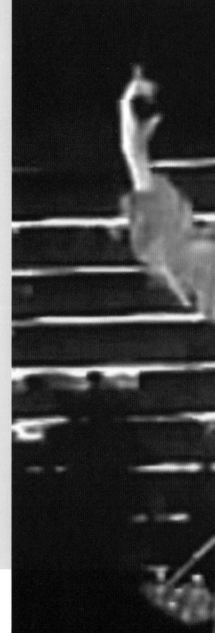

From the "Tell Me the Truth" tour, 2013.

"SINCE I'M VERY OPTIMISTIC ABOUT THE PEOPLE'S ABILITY TO CHANGE THE WORLD, THAT OPTIMISM IS GOING TO SHOW UP IN MY MUSIC."

95

PARTY MUSIC (2001)

# 5 MILLION WAYS TO KILL A CEO

We've got 5 million ways to kill a CEO
Slap him up and shake him up and then you know
Let him off the flo' then bait him with the dough
You can do it funk or do it disco
(2x)

Well I hope you testify
that it was worth your waitin
On the turf debatin
how to get it percolatin
He workin you while we happy just to work a Dayton
But I'mma slap him til my blood starts circulatin

Do your checks have elasticity?
Did they cut off yo lectricity?
Did you scream and yell explicitly?
Force the boss into complicity!

I'm a white chalk stencil
but I push a pencil
Rollin dope fiend rentals
through your residential
Broke as fuck
eatin lentils with no utensil
Finna teach pimp class
with a ho credential

They own sweatshops
pet cops
and fields of cola
Murder babies
with they molars on the areola
Control the Pope
Dali Lama
Holy Rollers
and the Ayatollah
Bump this rollin in your bucket or your new Corolla

Where you might catch me on the scenic route
with my penis out
Yellin, "Twamps for the executives with the meanest mouth!"
Wanna know what this demeanor's bout?

City tried to clean us out
Green is clout, shut 'em down
they ain't never seen a drought

You interviewed but they ain't callin you back
And for the record I ain't called it a gat
But tuck this in the small of your back
Wait in the bathroom stall 'til I tap

We've got 5 million ways to kill a CEO
Slap him up and shake him up and then you know
Let him off the flo' then bait him with the dough
You can do it funk or do it disco

Suck this game in slow
it's the creeper
If you's a janitor
get a street sweeper
Ugly is even skin deeper
If you cain't get the Prez
get the VeePer

They made the murder scene before there was a coroner
I mighta been born here
but I'm a foreigner
Spillin swigs
for victims of pigs
and Afeni's kid
Flip off the lid
who you pourin fo?

You too could be a corporate green killer
bean spiller
Gangster of Love
just like Steve Miller
They wear skivvies that's made of chinchilla
Factory in Mexico
bought a spring villa

I'm from the land where the Panthers grew
You know the city
and the avenue
If you the boss
we'll be smabbin through

and we'll be grabbin you
To say "Whassup with the revenue?"
And if you feel it we can even try to seal it with the

5 million ways to kill a CEO
Slap him up and shake him up and then you know
Let him off the flo' then bait him with the dough
You can do it funk or do it disco

Tell him it's a boom in child prostitution
When he show up at the stroll
give him lead restitution

You could throw a twenty in a vat o' hot oil
When he jump in after it
watch him boil

Toss a dollar in the river
and when he jump in
If you can find he can swim
put lead boots on him
and do it again!
You and a friend
Videotape and the party don't end

Tell him that boogers
be sellin like crack
He gon' put them little baggies in his nose
and suffocate like that

Put a fifty in the barrel of a gun
When he try to suck it out
(well you know this one)

Make sure you ain't got no priors
Don't tell 'em that we conspired
We could let him try to change a flat tire
Or we could all at once retire
There are just a few of the

5 million ways to kill a CEO
Slap him up and shake him up and then you know
Let him off the flo' then bait him with the dough
You can do it funk or do it disco

"I WOULD PROBABLY NOT MAKE A SONG ABOUT LITERALLY KILLING A CEO. NOT BECAUSE I HAVE A PROBLEM WITH IT PER SE, BUT BECAUSE THAT WOULDN'T BE A FUN SONG."

# WEAR CLEAN DRAWS

"Wear Clean Draws" is a song I wrote to my daughter just before her fourth birthday. When she was in fourth grade, the teacher gave them the assignment to bring in a recording of the song that they felt most spoke directly to them. So, of course, when she told me about the assignment, I said, "You have a song that is written directly to you." And she was like, "Daddy, I can't play that song, it's not appropriate for the fourth grade." And she was right, because the song is actually, even though I wrote it to her before her fourth birthday, meant for her for later.

So anyway, that's "Wear Clean Draws." On the recording her grandfather on her mother's side is actually whistling at the end, so that was a cool thing. Again, this is one of the first songs where I allowed myself to write about something emotional or personal because I always at first thought that that was not what I was here to do. But I wrote about things on a personal level, especially with this song, and left myself open to putting my ideas about everything into that subject, and my ideas about the world come through in that as well. — BOOTS

## WEAR CLEAN DRAWS

You know
you're my cookie baby and you're too smart
I can see it in the lines of your school art
True heart
I mean courage
Expressed with care
Go on draw them superheroes with the curly hair
You're my daughter
My love
More than kin to me
This for you and the woman that you finna be
Tell that boy he's wrong
Girls are strong
Next time at show and tell play him our song
Tell your teacher I said princesses are evil
How they got all they money was they killed people
If somebody hits you
Hit em back
Then negotiate a peace contract
Life is a challenge and you gotta team up
If you play house
pretend that the man clean up
You too busy with the other things you gotta do
If you start something, now
Remember
follow through
Later on you gon blossom like a lotus
You'll get into boys
and the boys gon notice
It don't matter who you do it with
Just remember when I tell you baby
you the shit
Handshakes are promises
Lies can spoil it
Words should be bond and seal
Wash your hands after using the toilet
Brush after every meal
And also

Wear clean draws
Everyday
Cuz things may fall
The wrong way
You'll be lying there
Waitin' for the ambulance
And your underwear

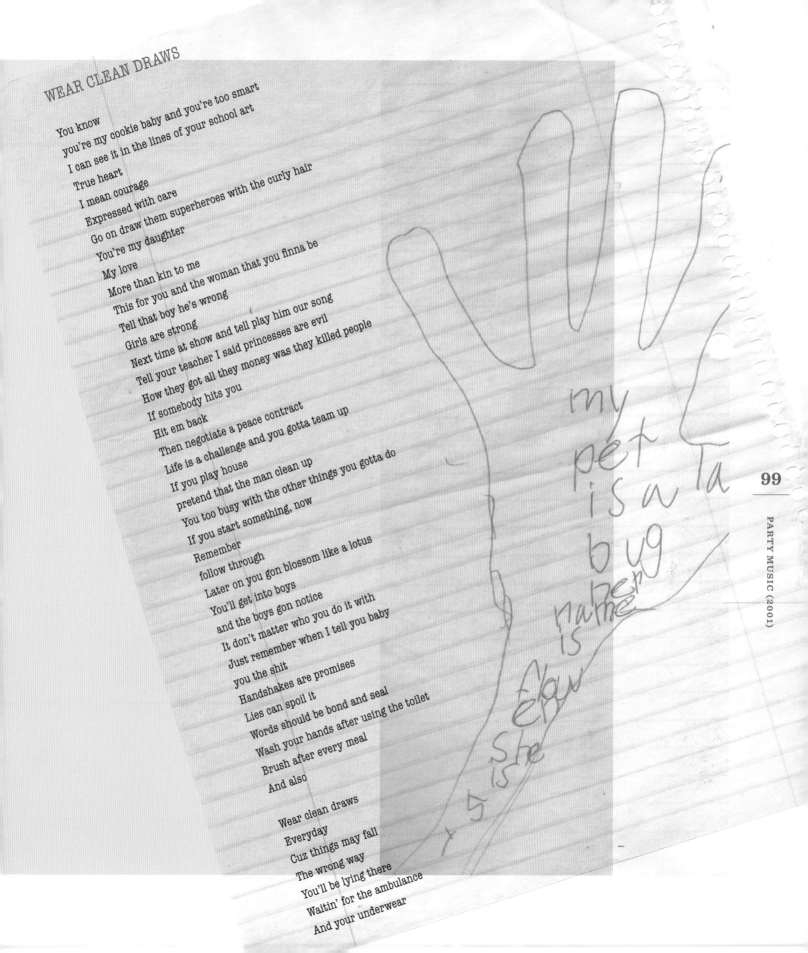

Got holes and shit
Wear clean draws
Everyday
Cuz things may fall
The wrong way
You'll be lying there
Waiting' for the ambulance
And your underwear
Got holes and shit

My boogie baby now
The world ain't no fairy tale
And it's ran by some rich white scary males
To make it simple for you
let's call em the bosses
They take money
while the people take losses
Stole Black folks from Africa
To work for free
And we still barely get paid enough to eat
That's what I told you
I be saying in my vocals
That's why the woman got the gun on the

logo
The star is the future
That we gon create
Where nobody steals money from the things
we make
The revolution takes time and space
But you
as a woman
gotta know your place:
That's in the front baby
I'm being blunt baby
If they get mad say it's they time of the
month baby
Your face is just like the sun when it raises
Thank you

for adding beauty to my phrases
Handshakes are promises
Lies can spoil it
Words should be bond and seal
Wash your hands after using the toilet
Brush after every meal
And like your grandaddy told me

Wear clean draws
Everyday
Cuz things may fall
The wrong way
You'll be lying there
Waiting' for the ambulance
And your underwear
Got holes and shit

BOOTS RILEY

Opposite page: *The Score* interview with
The Coup, April 2000.

# BURN, HOLLYWOOD, BURN!

BOOTS AND MEDUSA ON NATURAL HAIR DOS,
THE PERILS OF FLOSSIN', AND REPPIN' THE WEST
**INTERVIEW BY FRANK WILLIAMS**

> "EVERYONE IS SAYING IT HAS FEMINIST IDEAS IN IT BUT REALLY, IT IS JUST MY IDEAS FOR WHAT I WANT FOR MY DAUGHTER AND WHAT I WOULD WANT FOR ANYBODY."

**C**alifornia is known for gangsta raps. But saggin' and thuggin' ain't all the nation's most populous state has to offer. In the Bay Area, Oakland native Raymond Riley, better known as Boots of The Coup, has been kickin' revolutionary and socially conscious lyrics since we were in high school together in the late 1980s. His most recent record with DJ Pam The Funkstress is *Steal This Album* (Dog Day Records). Drive six hours south on the 5 freeway to South Central LA and you'll meet Medusa, who, like Boots, is a celebrated Cali MC whose soul-based style and old-school vibe has had major labels bitin' for years. In this exclusive interview, listen as they talk about their struggles to keep your brain and ass mov-

hop, aren't as popular on the West Coast?
**Medusa:** I think more than anything it's "How do we get her hits from hate rotation" that going on, and I like when people got a hold of something that's completely different than what's out there. Instead of looking at it as being something we'n originally say label as wack. I think we've just a little bit more political. But sometimes I think we underestimate our audience's intelligence and that's why they can't grasp what we're saying thinkin' they want as simple and political as possible.
**Boots:** Everything is politics. Even if you not trying to make a political song because any political meant life of how you got into any try to make my music talk about my life aspects.

they, to told you about your music?
**Medusa:** They say, "She's a star but she doesn't have an, songs that can fit into today's totality. What she's talking about is probably going to go over a lot of people's heads." And I don't feel like I'm talking too far out of anybody's range. When I do shows, young and old be up in the arenas and everybody's having a good time and recitin' my hooks. I mean, I don't feel like when you talking 'bout songs like "On Bad Sista" or "Finer Things (Black Eyed Peas and Collard Greens)?" What's so difficult about that?

**Boots:** But you have more floss is more relevant than the earthy things you rap about.
**Medusa:** What are you telling? This is Hollywood, baby. The way I look at it, like I'm sure Boots does, we tryin' to show that he is that we can still dress without havin' any, it's all in how genuine we are with our shit. 'Cause I'll rock some thrift store shit in a heartbeat and I'm trying to show younger sistas that you can still look good without trying to pay umpteen amount of thousands of dollars to get a fur and this and that and the other. I got me an old '64 Thunderbird. It's all in the way I carry myself as one bad sista.

**You both rock afros, Boots, why do you wear it?**
**Boots:** I had keep the 'fro and the sideburns so people would pick up the record and be like, "Oh, that's dope." I love the statement that I'm makin' with it. But it's not what's on your head. Whether you got a curl or a perm, whether you got short hair or long hair or whatever, the point is that what we are struggling for and what we are fighting for is the same thing. My appearance symbolizes something, but my appearance is secondary.

**Medusa:** I think it's a large part of rockin' your natural less is more too. I guess, but to bring that power and strength that was forgotten so we can remember it, familiarize ourselves with it and revive it.

**After listening to your lyrics, I can see how the feeling of camaraderie and brotha/sistahood goes hand in hand with the music.**
**Boots:** It's all about going deeper into what it's all about and when you do that, you come up with an answer. I'm not saying everybody needs to rap about revolution. But I think that people are looking for something more. A lot of the rappers are making formula songs. They may do something that sounds like they tryin' to reach people, you can tell that they never feel the song, but it got people going on a phone curls, him and, about that they

# GHETTO MANIFESTO

"Ghetto Manifesto" is actually the first song that I recorded on my own. **After we got the deal to do *Party Music*, I decided to spend the recording budget on buying my own studio, which I had been against doing up until this time.**

Before, in the '90s, many people who had their own studios were recording on ADATs and I really didn't like the sound of that. Before *Party Music*, all our music was recorded on two-inch magnetic tape. So it was analog, and I just felt that that sound was superior. I still like that sound better, but once I saw what you could do with Pro Tools, and the autonomy I would have to actually work on my stuff, I realized there was nothing better I could do with the advance money to record *Party Music* than buy my own studio.

Before that, I had only preproduction equipment. My preproduction equipment was nowhere near up to date. So I had an Atari 2600 computer that was synced up to samplers and keyboards, and through midi, I would program the samples and I would trigger the samples and keyboard things and we could record that like a player piano.

## GHETTO MANIFESTO

I write my lyrics on parking tickets
and summons to the court
I scribbled this
on an application for county support
I practice this like a sport
Met Donald Trump and he froze up
Standing on his Bentley yelling
"Pimps down, hos up"
Stop tryin to front off
Break our ass a clump off
We gon stop the world and
make y'all muthafuckas jump off
This is my resume/resignation
A ransom note

with proposed legislation
A fevered ultimatum
you should take it verbatim
Cause I got two bangin pieces and you don't
   wanna date em
Flyin kites for my folks at home
Who takin tokes alone
We payin rent on shit they ain't even
   sposed to own
Narratin' through my verse
agitatin you to curse
It's a million motherfuckers just waitin
   on the first
Anticipatin on the worst
wanna weighten up ya purse?
Shut the jobby job down at noon and don't
disperse
They wouldn't pay you as far as they could
   throw you
They think you punkin
but they don't know you
This is a turf operetta
played with twelve-shot berettas
By the Burger King workers
who be slappin on your lettuce
Wrote that
in the back of those apartments
On coupons
from agricultural departments
When we put down the X-O
we can let the threats go
And start shit
it's the ghetto manifesto

Call me bird cause of my legs
but my ass don't sing
Got a house arrest anklet
but it don't bling bling
Got a homie with a cell
but that shit don't ring
Cuz at lights out
bars clang and souls get stained

Now it's the hustler's soundtrack
where they muscle around blacks
Make your thoughts heavy
drop a jewel
and make the ground crack
Even renowned hack historians have
   found that
The people only bound back
when they pound back
So I take out a spray can
and pace the pavement
Deface engravements
of the sufferin they sent
The fouls are flagrant
and deaths the fragrance
I overheard them askin vagrants
for patience
So check the liner notes
I steal my finer quotes
From dope boys tryin to float
and bourgies in designer boats
And party liner jokes and all kind of folks
Who kind of broke
But bought twenties cause they feelin like
   a minor spoke
The trees we got lifted by
made our feet dangle
So when I say burn one I mean the Star-
   Spangled
Let's all get high
from the income angle
Bump this at the party
even if it ain't the single
Here's a slum serenade
on razor blades and grenades
By nannies and maids
who be polishin the suede
We could let the cess blow
but let's make the sets grow
Into brigades
with the ghetto manifesto

Then we'd go to the studio and lay all that stuff onto tape and then record live instruments over the synthesized parts or sometimes we might leave little sound samples in or whatever. But it was a tedious process and like I said, the Atari 2600 was already old when I started using it, for the first album, and it would often break down, and the last place that had Atari computer parts was in Oakland, luckily, but that closed down in '97 or '98. My computer would break down oftentimes recording *Steal This Album.* I would go to fire up the computer and it would take an hour to come on and an hour to get to the point that I would need to restart it. So often I would turn it on and be like, "Oh, I'm not working on music today."

So *Party Music* was a big step up. *Ghetto Manifesto* was my first experience just recording and I just asked my old engineer Matt Kelley for some technique tips on mic-ing. I camped out in my friend Degi Simmons's garage and he had a grand piano up in there and we would just record layer upon layer with musician friends and stuff like that. That's why that song has piano, bass, and then synthesizer, strings, and all kinds of percussion, because I was just trying to figure out how to do it.

There must have been like ninety-six different tracks to choose from at any point. And luckily I was able to carve it into this piece of music. The lyrics to this are pretty much just me going off in as close to freestyle fashion as I get. I came up with the first line, "I write my lyrics on parking tickets and summons to the court," because I was writing the lyrics on a parking ticket and there was a summons to the court right there, so I mean, it was pretty literal. —BOOTS

"SO I HAD AN ATARI 2600 COMPUTER THAT WAS SYNCED UP TO SAMPLERS AND KEYBOARDS, AND THROUGH MIDI, I WOULD PROGRAM THE SAMPLES AND I WOULD TRIGGER THE SAMPLES AND KEYBOARD THINGS AND WE COULD RECORD THAT LIKE A PLAYER PIANO."

GET UP

GET
UP

I wrote my verse for "Get Up" at the same time as STIC and M-1 wrote their verses. "Get Up" is originally with me and dead prez. dead prez is a group of folks who became my friends. I first met them in 1999. But I guess our history went back further, which is something I hadn't realized. The story goes like this: when we first started doing music we had something called the Mau Mau Rhythm Collective, which was a kind of loose-knit cultural organization of folks in Oakland who felt like we weren't able to get shows so we started throwing our own shows. And one of the reasons we thought we weren't able to get shows was because we spoke about political realities of what was going on around us, and that wasn't the style that clubs and promoters wanted to play at their venues.

So in answer to that we made the Mau Mau Rhythm Collective. Many of us who were artists were burnt-out organizers, people who had vowed to not organize for a while and just focus on our art. But as we did that, we grew in numbers. We started throwing shows that had to do with specific causes. One was in support of "welfare mothers" who were getting attacked by the court system. That was with the Women's Economic Agenda Project.

Then we'd have groups from all over Oakland and the Bay Area come—but the idea was that everybody perform-ed one song, and everybody's song had to do with whatever the subject was that month. So these grew in popularity; sometimes the subject was police brutality. One time the subject was the weed and seed program, which Oakland was trying to put in and did successfully.

But anyway, we'd do these things and we were strictly trying to be a cultural organization. Like I said, many of us had been organizers and being artists was kind of our

# GET UP

You got to get up right now
Turn the system upside down
You sposed to be fed up right now
Turn the system upside down
Get up!

You got to get up right now
Turn the system upside down
You sposed to be fed up right now
Turn the system upside down
Get up!

[STIC]:

Honestly
I'm against this government
I ain't gotta cover it up
that's what I meant
Sick of payin bills and I'm sick of payin rent
Seem like I work all the time
but don't know where the money went
And the funny shit is
we sposed to like this shit
But all y'all politicians can bite this dick
It's a war goin on
the ghetto is a cage
They only give you two choices
be a rebel or a slave
(So what you do?)
So I rebel
Like a ulcer
in the belly of the beast
stayin true to it
Since my Houghton Street days in the blue
Buick
Niggas been fightin so long
seem like I'm used to it
Now what y'all know 'bout how The Coup
do it?
Truth fluid
Boots put the funk to it
ain't nothin to it
This is for the Gs
all the way to the bay
From 'Frisco to Oakland
all over L.A.
you gotta get up

[Boots]:

Now uh,
this fella's
piss yella
never been a snitch teller
One pay stub from a homeless ditch dweller
Yellin "Fuck a Rocafella!"
my shit bump in acapella
My lyrical quotes
are nervous notes
to bank tellers
Sayin "Call it off, we haulin off Molotovs and
bricks"
Mr. Bailiff
you can put that in the transcipts
Hope your motherfuckin paddy wagon van
flips
Some saw it off
I prefer hand-grips
Quote us
you know we're stronger than a 3-day
notice
Pay or quit
It's more of us than lies your mayor spit
I'm on some
I-hate-the-game-but-love-the-player shit
Is you a have or you a have-not?
When you run out of bullets
grab rocks
Cuz the prison door slam locks
It don't open when your fam knocks
Unless you rich and have stocks
Fight the power
like a motherfuckin Zulu
It's The Coup

escape from that, but the people that joined called bullshit and asked why we weren't organizing around these things, asking why we were just getting people to make music about it and why weren't we joining these community organizations that were doing things, much to the chagrin of the folks that founded the Mau Mau Rhythm Collective, of which I was one. We got talked into becoming more of a political organization and we did join in many of those campaigns.

When we started the Mau Mau Rhythm Collective and started doing shows and things like that in conjunction with organizations, many ex–Black Panthers came to us and said, "Great! I've been looking for something to get my son or daughter involved in that had a political angle to it. I'm glad you guys are doing this, here's my kid, when's the meeting?" And many of those folks forced us to be more active and more political.

Niko Slater was one of these Panther children and Niko was very instrumental in making the Mau Mau Rhythm Collective happen. I think that as The Coup got popular and I was gone more often, the Mau Mau Rhythm Collective started to not be as active, and then it really became not so active once Niko left.

Anyway, Niko went away to school at Florida A&M and she said she was going to start up a chapter of the Mau Mau Rhythm Collective out there. I'm not sure what happened, but every Saturday I'd get a call from somebody who was kicking it at her house. I don't know if they were having a meeting or whatever, and it would be a two-hour-long discussion about a lot of things, but you know we had a video at the time, so a lot of times it would be about the music industry, because this guy was doing

GET UP (CONTINUED)

plus Knumh and Mutulu
So raise your hands in the air
like you're born again
But make a fist
for the struggle we was born to win

You got to get up right now
Turn the system upside down
You sposed to be fed up right now
Turn the system upside down
Get up!

[M-1]:

When I hear the woop-woop
I be duckin them hos
I can smell a pig comin
so I stay on my toes
On the low from po-po
so fuck the Ho-lice
Cuz peace to me
is loaded under my seat
And I know power respects that
so "serve and protect" that
I'm young, black, and just don't give a fuck—
try me
Grillin you right back
you better drive by me
We the People Army
is known to get rowdy
And even if you a friend of the blue
You can get it too
snitchin is never forgettable
This Hell we livin is never forgivable

It come down to DP and The Coup
Remember Huey, Bobby Hutton, George,
Fred and them
Fuck the po-po
local, state, fed and them
You better choose your side
Crip
Blood
415
It's one team
get up and let's ride!

You got to get up right now
Turn the system upside down
You sposed to be fed up right now
Turn the system upside down
Get up!

music and wanted to know about it.

For a good six to eight months this happened. Every Saturday I'd get this call and you know, since this was through Niko I'd talk to this guy, because apparently they were going to form this organization.

Anyway, I stopped talking to the guy and in 1999 I go to New York to kick it, to meet dead prez for the first time. By the way, like I'd said before, I'd quit doing music after *Genocide and Juice* and started an organization with some friends called The Young Comrades, which was an organization with ideas to focus on issues that were going on in the Black community, but coming at it with a class-conscious, internationalist perspective.

Anyway, one day when we were cleaning out The Young Comrades' office, and this must have been in like '97, I heard a compilation tape that had a song called "Food, Clothes, and Shelter" by dead prez. I had kind of given up on music, but I heard that, and I was kind of like, "Wow, these dudes are doing it." And it inspired me, and that's one of the many reasons I went back and recorded *Steal This Album.*

So, after *Steal This Album,* I went to meet with dead prez, and we were going to record a song for a compilation that never came out. Within the first hour of my sitting with them (at the time dead prez was three people—STIC, M-1, and their producer, Tahir) Tahir said, "Yeah, like you said, blah blah blah and blah blah blah." It was something that apparently I had said, and it sounded like something I would say, but I was like, "When did I say that to you?" and he was like, "You said that back when we used to always call you on the phone, every week back in the day."

We hit it off, and there were very few people in the

music industry that I had ever come across who had an approach to songwriting with the same motivations. And finally I had found people good at what they do, and who I could relate to. So we'd made a few attempts at songs together. They didn't come out for whatever reason. As a matter of fact, we had a group together called The Instigators. We always went in the studio and it never worked out, but this is the song that we have. This was almost—I think the idea at first was that this would be a part of The Instigators album, and STIC said, "Boots put the funk to it" because he wrote the verse to my original beat. But I didn't like the original beat, and I asked Tahir to make a beat for it that was really good. And that's the beat you hear, the one Tahir did.

**Alright, that's "Get Up."** — BOOTS

# RIDE THE FENCE

Insets: stills from the music video for "Ride the Fence."

# RIDE THE FENCE

I'm anti-imperial
anti-trust
anti-gun if the shit won't bust
anti-corporate
they anti-my essence
anti-snortin them anti-depressants
but i'm not pro-poppin' em;
i'm provocative
and pro-stoppin them FBI operatives
who professional at Black Man Pounce
and hand you a sentence that you can't pronounce
I'm also anti-narco
anti-vice
911 marks the anti-christ
they anti-social
pointin' M-16s
guess i'm anti-the-anti-nigger-machine
Proletarianfunkadelicparliamentarian
pro-revolt-in-the-21st-centurian
pro-running up in Congress sayin "fuck it all!"
but bring the people with you
that's the protocol
This beat is joyful like jailbreaks
the whole world
is anti-United Snakes
so check it out
anticipate the anti-venom
and move your antibodies to this revolution rhythm
we gon be fuckin with em
pro-union but most lost they bite
anti-muthafuckas crossin a strike
take a look around
and be for or against
but you can't do shit if you ridin' the fence.

Ride the fence
now you don't really wanna
ride the fence
now do you really wanna
ride the fence?
why would you really wanna

ride the fence
don't ride the fence.
Ride the fence
now you don't really wanna
ride the fence
now do you really wanna
ride the fence?
why would you really wanna
ride the fence
don't ride the fence.

I'm anti-uppin-your-dollars-with-telekinesis
(I done tried every day, and that shit decreases)
Anti-them-anti-crime-bill-pieces
We need cash and that's the anti-thesis
I'm pro-overthrow of the "Hip-Hop Nation"
pro-layin'-low-til-I'm-off-probation
pro-people's-control-of-the-cash-of-corporations
pro-prophylactic yet pro-creation
anti-watered-down-drinks-in-fancy-cups
anti-promoters-who-don't-ante-up
but I'm not anti-club
I know that power is the most effective anti-drug
I'm pro-Zapatista
pro-Cuba
Viva!
Pro-la raza sayin "fuck la migra!"
policia se asesina
lemme show you what I mean
I'm anti-republican and democratic
if they self-destruct
that's anti-climactic
tired of bein hunted like an antelope
take the system by the throat
that's the antidote
so I pose a proposition
take a look
be in support or opposition
then be proactive proceed with confidence
cause you know that you can't change shit by ridin' the fence

Ride the fence
now you don't really wanna (7x)

# NOWA-LATERS

"Nowalaters" is pretty much a true story of something that happened to me when I was seventeen, and again, a lot of times I'll make music and I'll just kind of sit with it and see what emotion the music gives to me. I felt like the music was nostalgic and somewhat melancholic but with a hint of hopefulness in it. So I wrote about my process of coming to terms with what happened. Now every single thing in the precise way didn't happen—I'm not making a documentary and trying to spell it out exactly as it happened. I'm still an artist.

But pretty much it's what went down, and it had to do with my coming to terms with and understanding later the situation that created the incident. In short, if you're too lazy to read the lyrics, a girl I was with claimed that she was pregnant by me, and it turned out to not be true, and not only was it not true, she was pregnant before

# NOWALATERS

Well
if you thrust
eventually you gon gush
And I'm implyin' I ain't had no business cryin
Cause we used the rubber twice
And we knew that shit was dyin to bust
Well, we was only seventeen
But you was older in between
And in my fresh Adidas fits
I used to come more clean than Jeru jerkin off in a can of
chlorine
Sophisticated with the game I was spittin' in
A nymphomaniac but with less discipline
or experience
"V" on my chest—
When I was put to the test
You said "God damn nigga, that ain't how you get it in"
Dashboards for leverage—
Tall cans for beverage
The weed can make you courageous—
Make a Honda Civic seem so spacious—
Make five minutes seem like ages—
anyway

You smelled like Care-Free Curl—
And Nowalaters, baby
Said you liked—
High-top fades
And Jesse Johnson's "Crazy"
Seventeen—
all on you
like chicken and some gravy
Learned a lot
thank you much—
today I'm still campaignin

The lake don't smell so bad now, do it?
Don't trip off yo hair baby just re-glue it
The windows is fogged up
cain't nobody view it
Put down the Old E—

and turn up the Howard Hewitt
In some months—
we had things to discuss
Like how we blew it, we got amniotic fluid
And a baby floatin' through it
Hey, imagine if it look like us
it was me up in the vaginary
And I'ma love my kids—
whether real or imaginary
Quit school—
work at World O' Pants at the mall—
next to Fashion Berry
Operation Cash'n'Carry
Manual labor from six to noon
Makin' six doubloons
got a baby that's finsta bloom
And he needs fits to groom—
plus grits to spoon
So let me twist a plume
inhale—
and emit the fumes

You smelled like Care-Free Curl—
And Nowalaters, baby
Said you liked—
High-top fades
And Jesse Johnson's "Crazy"
Seventeen—
all on you
like chicken and some gravy
Learned a lot
thank you much—
today I'm still campaignin

I was composed—
I didn't even crack a frown
I was supposed
to let my pants fall down
And show my ass when I found
That the baby was four months early—
and around ten pounds
I heard a lot of bad things about teenage mothers
From those who don't really give a fuck about life

she met me. There are a lot of songs about this, right, but the fact is that I realized that the people around her had brought her up to think that the most important thing in her life was to be with a man.

That clearly there was no way that she could survive being a woman with a child, that's what they taught her. So, she was really scared, and this unfortunate situation happened. Again, as I say in the song, I didn't look at it that way right then, but this song was me coming to terms with that.

The references in the chorus, "you smelled like Care-Free Curl and Nowalaters baby," are literally true. It's from back when I had a hi-top fade and I was a big fan of Prince and Jesse Johnson. Anyway, that's that song. I want to add that a lot of times when we look at our memories, when something terrible happens or something bad happens, the unfortunate thing is that we forget all the good stuff. And I wanted to write a song that didn't only remember the bad things about that relationship, that remembered it correctly. And if I had remembered that time correctly, I would have no choice but to look at my actions as humorous and full of fault. No choice but to look at the time as being somewhat magical. I hope the addition of Mike Auberg's lead synth playing on that song contributed to that feeling too. I threw in those after I wrote the lyrics. — BOOTS

## NOWALATERS [CONTINUED]

They say "It ain't so much that they startin' out younger"
"It's just—they supposed to be more like a wife"
Meanin' "you ain't shit without a man to guide you"
If your mama tried to feed you that—
she lied too
Make ya grab any motherfucka that ride through
If jobs are applied to
knots can get tied too
Plus I know that you musta been scared
It made it easy when them feelings were shared
Flashbacks are 20/20
I know you wasn't for the dollars
cause you knew I had funny money
Yellin' all loud like I'mma tear the whole hood up
You said leave—
cause the real daddy stood up
You said I was a mark for believin' in you
Now it's more that I'm seein' is true
There's a few things I'd like to say in this letter
Like I wish I would've seen him grow
And ask my wife I learned to fuck much better
And—
thank you for lettin' me go
Yeah, thank you—
for lettin' me go
For real—
thank you for lettin' me go

You smelled like Care-Free Curl—
And Nowalaters, baby
Said you liked—
High-top fades
And Jesse Johnson's "Crazy"
Seventeen—
all on you
like chicken and some gravy
Learned a lot
thank you much—
today I'm still campaignin

# "I DIDN'T LOOK AT IT THAT WAY RIGHT THEN, BUT THIS SONG WAS ME COMING TO TERMS WITH THAT."

# PORK AND BEEF

"In the music studio in my house in West Oakland which I lived and worked in for a few years. This is where we did *Pick a Bigger Weapon*. It's also where Beyoncé did her first album." — BOOTS

"CAPITALISM-BASHING COP-HATING RAPPER BOOTS RILEY IS BACK."

~ MICHELLE MALKIN, ON OCCUPY OAKLAND, NOVEMBER 2, 2011

# PORK AND BEEF

If you got beef with C-O-Ps
Throw a Molotov at the P-I-Gs
Cause they be harassing you and
me
Ya gotta understand that we still
not free (2x)

[Boots]:

This is for them babies
with them empty plates
For that raised rent rate
you didn't calculate
If you ever in your life
been a ward of the state
On the corner with cake
If they sent an undercover and
you took
　　the bait
Next time I see em
with no hesitation
I'm peeling off like stolen registration
And leave a dart of smoke
See I'm that sort of folk
That they been hunting
since my mama's fucking water
broke
Cause they the henchmen
nah
they the lynchpin
Between the rich and po

so we don't entrench them
and say "Dispense with the dollars
and cents
Or where you stand gon be
candles, flowers,
　　and incense!"
Behind steel gates
is fifty-cent-a-hour bill rates
Up in Quentin
making microchips for Bill Gates
Pelican Bay
t-shirts for the workout
Police station
where the slave catchers lurk out
Let's let the thunder out
no more taking under routes
We'll synchronize
and then give em' shit to wonder
bout
The DA is filthy
yell not guilty
We need control of the cash and
the realty
And get rid of all the motherfuck-
ing
　　parasites
More than weed burns at 420
Fahrenheit
Shaking in they boots when we
start to bust
They ain't scared of rap music
they scared of us

If you got beef with C-O-Ps

Throw a Molotov at the P-I-Gs
Cause they be harassing you and
me

# HEVEN TONIGHT

BOOTS RILEY

"Outside of Soulbeat TV Studios in 1993, on Foothill Boulevard, in Oakland. Pam was a regular DJ on *Soulbeats Hip-hop Slam*." —BOOTS

I wrote this chorus because, while we were mixing *Party Music,* Meshell Ndegeocello was mixing her album *Cookie: The Anthropological Mixtape* and she said she was down to come be on the album. **So we quickly went to my studio, made up some music and wrote a chorus that I thought fit her cadence. She never came, she faked. She's a good friend of mine, and I hope she's reading this, because she's not on the album because she faked.**

**Anyway, the song is pretty clear what it's about. I call it "Heven Tonite," because I think that instead of waiting for heaven after you die, we should make heaven right here. A lot of the ways that I form the verses are, in my mind, related to certain prayers and things like that, definitely the beginning of it. The beginning of the first verse is obviously that way.**

**And this is making me remember something about "Everythang." So the last two songs of *Party Music* that were to be recorded were "Heven Tonite" and something else. I had lied to the record label telling them that the**

# HEVEN TONITE

Preacher man wanna save my soul
Don't nobody wanna save my life
People we done lost control
Let's make heaven tonite
Preacher man wanna save my soul
Don't nobody wanna save my life
People we done lost control
Let's make heaven tonite

Now as I sleep may the oxygen inflate my
    lungs
May my arteries and heart oscillate as one
If police come
may I awake
escape
and run
In the morning may I have the sake to
    scrape the funds
And if I take the plunge
May it be said that I wasn't afraid to
    shake my tongue
Show the state was scum
Makin sure that the callin bell of fate was
rung
Cuz if they could they would
And probly tried to
Rape the sun
Someone said that this is just my body
Wait for the Afterparty
Where ain't no shut-off note
And every wallet there is knotty
Feet are on the asphalt
Dick in the dirt
This system take vickin to work
Listen alert
Check out the introvert
In the corner with the rip in her skirt
Stomach pains so she grippin her shirt
Ain't never had dinner
So she know she ain't gettin dessert
Don't try to tell me it's her mission to hurt

I got faith in the people and they power
    to fight
We gon make the struggle blossom
Like a flower to light
I know that we could take power tonight
Make em cower from might
And get emergency clearance from the
    tower for flight
I ain't sittin in your pews less you helpin
    me resist and refuse
Show me a list of your views
If you really love me
Help me tear this muthafucka up
Consider this my tithe for the offer cup

Preacher man wanna save my soul
Don't nobody wanna save my life
People we done lost control
Let's make heaven tonite
Preacher man wanna save my soul
Don't nobody wanna save my life
People we done lost control
Let's make heaven tonite

I used to think about infinity
And how my memory is finna be
Invisibly slim in that vicinity
And though the stars are magnificent
Whisky and the midnight sky can make
    you feel insignificant
The revolution in this tune and verse
Is a bid for my love to touch the universe
Strugglin over wages and funds
Let the movement get contagious and run
Through the end when it's gauges and guns
And if we win in the ages to come
We'll have a chapter where the history
    pages are from
They won't never know our name or face
But feel our soul in free food they taste
Feel our passion when they heat they house
When they got power on the streets
And the police don't beat 'em about

Let's make health care centers on every
    block
Let's give everybody homes and a garden
    plot
Let's give all the schools books
Ten kids a class
And give 'em truth for their pencils and pads
Retail clerk—"love ballads" where you place
this song
Let's make heaven right here
Just in case they wrong

Preacher man wanna save my soul
Don't nobody wanna save my life
People we done lost control
Let's make heaven tonite
Preacher man wanna save my soul
Don't nobody wanna save my life
People we done lost control
Let's make heaven tonite

album was almost done, way before, when I only really had three songs done, so a lot of these were songs that I forced myself to get done by the deadline.

But when I finished the album I felt like it was missing a song. It was missing a certain feeling, you know, something that was more aggressive. The record label had already—because they thought the album was done way before—they had already bought the ticket for me to go master the album, and if I didn't master the album on this certain day and certain time, I wasn't going to be able to get in, and we'd have to push the album back to the next year. It was sort of a weird thing.

But I had two hours to get on my plane and be in New York by the next day and master the album. I listened to the whole album and felt like it was missing something. I found the music to "Everythang" on my hard drive which I never wrote any lyrics for. Didn't have a concept or anything and it just happens to be that was one of the quickest songs that I've ever written and it's, like I said earlier, one of my favorite songs to perform.

We recorded the vocals and added some extra synth stuff on top of it, and mixed it down in two hours including while I was writing it. I even made it to my flight. This was before September 11, 2001, so you could get to the airport really late. I got to the plane with the master recording in my hand, got there five minutes before the plane took off, and it all worked out. Luckily that last-minute push gave me a song that I really like—not only is it on *Party Music*, but we did a cover of it on Street Sweeper Social Club *The Ghetto Blaster EP*. —BOOTS

THOUGHT ABOUT IT 2

Have you thought about it too?
Because we are here for you
When you have nothing to lose
All the people feel it too

You do have a way out baby
And together we can breathe free air

Have you thought about it too?
Because we are here for you
When you have nothing to lose
All the people feel it too

I know they wanna isolate you
Give you nothing to relate to
We're gonna have to break this whole muthafucka down

So
Loneliness
Don't let it overtake you

When you feel so all alone
Know you have a home

# LAZY-MUTHA-FUCKA

This is a song that I wrote to counter the idea that poor people are the laziest people. We get told that quite often as a rationale for why the system is the way it is. Why the rich have all the money, and why the rest of us don't. We're taught that part of the reason is because when you work hard you get rich, and when you don't you don't. So I wanted to shed light on the folks that—and I'm talking about the superrich, I'm not even just talking about the CEO of a company—but I'm talking about the billionaires who were born into money and didn't have to work to get there.

I'm talking about the folks that have an assistant to do every little thing that they have to do. And the folks that have butlers and maids to accomplish what they need to get done. We don't see that as lazy for some reason in this society, and there are many of you who will read this and

# LAZYMUTHAFUCKA

Now when I go to bed
it's almost time to wake up
Tryin not to go to jail
tryin not to cake up
And even when I served soda up
it would be cold as fuck
Shiverin in my socks
servin knocks for ten bucks
And you be in the house
all warm and shit
In a Ascot sweater with the fire lit
And whatever you want
you ain't gotta lift a finger
If you want a glass of water
hit the maid on the ringer
Got a job from you
under this hot ass sun
You tellin me to hurry up and get some
    mo shit done
I be so tired
when I speak all my word slur together
Got so many calluses my hands are like
leather
Watchin MTV in yo big ass chair
Tryin out slang words while you combin
    your hair
"Your productivity's wack"
"Bring that box here forsheezy"
"Go get some coffee player"
"Punch out before you leave me"
Got your feet up on the desk
noddin off to sleep
While I lift, push, pull, dig, sweat, and sweep
I could work hard all my life
and in the end still suffer
Cause the world is controlled by you lazy
    muthafuckas

You's a lazy muthafucka, lazy muthafucka
You's a lazy muthafucka, lazy muthafucka

Now you don't wash your ass

you got a personal bather
If you roll out of bed it's like you doin' a favor
You was born into paper
and that behavior
For a midnight snack
you have the bedroom catered
You ain't never learned to drive
or tie your shoe
I got my ear to the street and my eye on you
You got a secretary
to write down your thoughts
On how to make us work hard
and fatten up your vaults
TV say if you poor
you must be slow and shiftless
But you pay 'em to say that so we don't
    want it different
Got a cook
and a girl to bring the tray for you
You hearin this
cause somebody pushed play for you
My head is poundin now
and my hands are shakin
To keep my eyelids open takes concentratin
I don't get no rest
it's just a stay alive hustle
Making you stay rich without you moving a
muscle
You think of people as your tool
So when your dick salute
You have the butler get the phone
and call a prostitute
And say "Your sex drive's stronger than the
engine of a trucker"
But she'll have to be on top
cause you's a lazy motherfucker

You's a lazy muthafucka, lazy muthafucka
You's a lazy muthafucka, lazy muthafucka

A hundred person house staff just to
    sanitize you
know you don't give a fuck but they all
despise you

Millions over millions
makin shit for you to sell
Got police on alert just in case we rebel
But it's gon' happen cap'n
hope you know that's why I'm rappin
Want the toes to start tappin
hands and gats to start clappin
Cause this whole system works
for you to kick it in Paris
Or roll through Hong Kong in a rickshaw
    carriage
So when you spend a dollar
that's ten seconds of my time
And when you spend a billion
that's my life and that's a crime
Cause to me life is hard like the track that
    I'm reppin on
Callin' for the freedom of the backs that you
    steppin on
Later for the "pull-up-your-bootstraps" factor
Cause hard work got me to the chiropractor
But we can work hard
to take back the bread and butter
Cause all these multimillionaires is lazy
motherfuckers

You's a lazy muthafucka, lazy muthafucka
You's a lazy muthafucka, lazy muthafucka

think that that doesn't exist. As a matter of fact, I think Robert Christgau, who usually likes a lot of our work, you know, his big critique—it's almost like he got mad, when it came to this song—his big critique was that the super-rich are not lazy, they're megalomaniacs.

And that may be true for some of them, but many of them were born into money and live a pretty fat, luxurious lifestyle. And they have pet projects, they do work and do things that they are interested in doing, much in the way that folks that have a hobby collecting baseball cards work at that. In this case they work with millions of dollars on projects and companies that they throw money into.

Anyway, these folks are, you know, pretty damn lazy. Lazymuthafucka. — BOOTS

London, 2000.

# "I'M TALKING ABOUT THE BILLIONAIRES WHO WERE BORN INTO MONEY AND DIDN'T HAVE TO WORK TO GET THERE."

# STEAL THIS ALBUM (1998)

70895-234134-7

1. THE SHIPMENT
2. ME AND JESUS THE PIMP IN A '79 GRANADA LAST NIGHT
3. 20,000 GUN SALUTE
4. BUSTERISMOLOGY
5. CARS AND SHOES
6. BREATHING APPARATUS
7. THE REPO MAN SINGS FOR YOU
8. U.C.P.A.S.
9. UNDERDOGS
10. SNEAKIN' IN
11. PISS ON YOUR GRAVE
12. FIXATION

# STEAL THIS ALBUM

After *Genocide and Juice,* I was tired of being an artist. I wanted to go back to organizing. I quit doing music and some friends and I started an organization called The Young Comrades. We were involved in some grassroots campaigns, but after a couple years it devolved into little more than a study group. I figured that if all we were gonna do is put out ideas, I could do that much better and on a wider scale through my music.

This is when I started working on *Steal This Album.* I had worked out a 50/50 deal with Dogday Records, where they would pay for studio time, but they didn't have the resources to pay for anything else. So the players on the album are all friends who just wanted to see me put out some more music. Some of the players were actually in The Young Comrades. Others were professional musicians who also were my friends. We made this whole album for half the price of our first music video.

It was on this album that we first started printing the lyrics in the liner notes. I think this caused critics to go back and look at our albums in a different way. Before this album, we got very little coverage from journalists.

— BOOTS

# THE SHIPMENT

It ain't Indonesia
China White
Purple-Haired Thai
Big H Delight
Take my shit we gon have to fight
I'm always rollin dirty
so be actin right
It ain't Indonesia
China White
Purple-Haired Thai
Big H Delight
Take my shit we gon have to fight
I'm always rollin dirty
so be actin right

I'm bombing uppercut swipes
as my knuckles ignite
More strikes
than a teachin staff's fight for pay hikes
Like cleats with spikes
I clings to my turf tight
Get low like a Smurf might
earth is my birthright
You salivate at the sound of the bell
I come sick
and make your lymph nodes swell
Nickel-plated teeth and tongue as well
so you can tell
when I'm shootin' off my mouth
the politicians start to bail
When I shoot
Fuhrmans scoot
I'm yellin "Gimme all the loot!"
Bourgeoisie
pimpin me
now my digits don't compute
Chillin in the house of ill repute
But is you wearin canvasols
or purple-pinstripe suits?
Fact of earth and comets:
macroeconomics

Yak until you vomit
or come up on a lick
Sweat oozin out my skin
just to get another fin
Changed my name to Valerie
so I can get WIC
Savage Storm Troopers be less than seducin
Jailtime producin
silly Lilliputians!
This Gulliver comes equipped with a 4-4
and twelve comrades in a box Chev 4-do
Skirtin down the strip with a mission to render
And we don't give a fuck if we missin a fender
Mix it in a blender
you ain't home
return to sender
Can't be saved by cokenders
or a public defender
This ain't no macrobiotic chemical colonic
This politicalsymphoniclyricalnarcotic
Somethin much mo potent that we plotted
Come and get some
if you ain't got it

It ain't Indonesia
China White
Purple-Haired Thai
Big H Delight
Take my shit we gon have to fight
I'm always rollin dirty
so be actin right
It ain't Indonesia
China White
Purple-Haired Thai
Big H Delight
Take my shit we gon have to fight
I'm always rollin dirty
so be actin right

Ex-ex-ex-ex-ex-exhilarating!
I accuse you of N-hating!
And exploitating for profit making
don't cop a plea

cause I'm B-double-O-T, from the C-O-U the P

I feel my epidermis

at its firmest

just before a skirmish

If you want green like Kermit

keep it heated like a Thermos

Aspire to be famous

puttin fire in their anus

Made the rulin class hate us

more than child support payments

to Rosemary's Baby

shick-a-shick-shady!!

Pissin' in your gumbo

and they tell you, "It's all gravy!"

Cuz you can't trust a big grip and a smile

And I slang rocks—

but Palestinian style

Now there's a rumble in the jungle

never mumble though I humble

Couple rappers took a tumble

but my folks still want the bumble

Who's pimpin your bundle?

I'm fly like Seth Brundle

If you're snitchin to Columbo

we gon drop you like a fumble

Now what you make is point-oh-one percent

of what the boss make

And what the boss take

is keepin' us from livin great

If this ain't straight

you think you wanna sit down and negotiate

You better have a crew

to help you shut down his estate

Don't get frustrated—

Discombobulate it!

Don't stand and debate it—

get a mob and take it!

Til then it's food stamps

Vouchers

mildew-smellin couches

Overturned garbage cans

wit no Oscar the Grouches

Makin money sellin plastic pouches

As Mystikal would say

"My flo is covered wit roaches!"

Absotively

Posolutely

can't do without it

The Shipment is delivered

come and get it if you bout it!


It ain't Indonesia

China White

Purple-Haired Thai

Big H Delight

Take my shit we gon have to fight

I'm always rollin dirty

so be actin right

It ain't Indonesia

China White

Purple-Haired Thai

Big H Delight

Take my shit we gon have to fight

I'm always rollin dirty

so be actin right


Systematic playa-hation

Green paper complications

Got my ass an education

Can I get an application?

# ME AND JESUS THE PIMP IN A '79 GRANADA LAST NIGHT

So this is about "me and Jesus the pimp." I wanted to write a song about sexism and I don't think I had done that so specifically before. However, I know that my experience is different from women's and I could not really write about sexism honestly, just from the standpoint that sexism hurts women. I could do that objectively and theoretically, but it would be hard to make a real song about it that felt honest, at least emotionally. And I saw a lot of people trying to do this at the time, and years before, but it felt like they were blatantly making a "message song," which at least by that time, I had tried to stop doing, unless I was just going over the top with it to be you know, funny, or whatever. So with this song, I decided I was going to need to tell a story about how sexism against women affects men. I also didn't only want to talk about sexism.

This was kind of a mentally masturbatory piece for

## ME AND JESUS THE PIMP IN A '79 GRANADA LAST NIGHT

Well

he was smilin like a vulture

as he rolled up the horticulture

Ignited it

and said, "I hope the vapors don't insult ya"

What I replied denied

but he mixin weed and hop

His head was noddin up and down

like he agreed a lot

Bored

said, "We need a plot"

I comply, "Let's leave the spot"

Hopped in the Granada

he's impressed by the beat I got

His name is [Hay-soos]

but his pimp name is [Gee-zus]

Slapped a hoe to pieces

with his plastic prosthesis

"Nigga don't you know that I'm your daddy?"
      said he

This is true

plus he schooled me for my mackin' degree

"Never plea

try not to flee

make niggas pee when you stick around"

This man my momma had found

taught me to put it down

I press the gas to the ground

to show that I'm a hound

Make sure that "get-rubber" sound

is heard throughout the town

Thirty years ago

Jesus could pull a ho quick

But now he 50

and his belly hangs lower than his dick

Philosophy that he spit

stuck in my memory chips

And now he puttin in a disk

of Gladys Knight and the Pips

Then that shit starts to skip

he said, "Somebody musta scratch it"

Put the 40 to his lips

and poured the contents

down the hatchet

Well

since my adolescence

cause of his pimp lessons

smack my woman in the dental just for askin'
      silly questions

Relationship reduction

to either rock the box

or suction

Ain't got no close patnahs

socially

I can't function

From the pen he would scribe

on how to survive:

"Don't be Microsoft

be Macintosh

with a Hard Drive"

Used to tell me all the time

to keep a bitch broke

Did I mention

that my momma was his number one ho?

Clunked the 40 on the flo

and placed his palm on the dash

and wheezed out

"C'mon man

make this motherfucker mash!"

Ain't gon' mash too fast

cause my tags ain't right

Me and Jesus the Pimp in a '79 Granada
      last night

Oakland do you wanna ride?

I can't hear you! Oakland do you wanna
      ride tonight? (2x)

City lights

from far away

can make you drop your jaw

Sparklin

like sequins on a transvestite at Mardi Gras

There's beauty

in the cracks of the cement

When I was five

I hopped over them wherever we went

to prevent

whatever it was

that could break my momma's back

Little did I know

that it would roll up in a Cadillac

And matter fact

she couldn't see him like a cataract

And on the track

she went from beautiful

to battle-axe

And back at home

she would cry into her pillow

Vomit in the commode

I was six years old

I would crawl onto her lap

and we would hug and hold

Never knew how she was sufferin for my
      food and clothes

She asked me what I thought of Jesus

when he broke off some bread

I said

"He missin a arm

and he seem like a pee-pee head"

She said

"Don't cuss"

and my teeth to go brush

And get ready for bed

and the toilet to flush

With tears in my momma's eyes

I was her everything

Before she went out on the stroll

She'd tuck me into bed

and sing:

You're much too beautiful for words (4x)

me, because I wanted to do a lot of things in it literarily, that maybe wouldn't lead to the song being good, but I just wanted to know that I did it. So I wanted to talk about sexism and capitalism, and I wanted the lyrics to allude to other things in the real world. So first off, the title "Me and Jesus the Pimp in a '79 Granada Last Night," could have easily been "Me and Jesus the Pimp in a '64 Impala Last Night," which is probably what I thought of first, I actually don't remember. But, I wanted it to be a regular car, and something not so flashy, but I also wanted the song, in my talk about capitalism, to have something to do with revolution. And this is where I messed up, because I thought, I knew that there was a car called the Granada, and actually I'd had one before, and I knew that there had been a socialist revolution in Granada and I wanted to make the connection. I thought that socialist revolution in Granada was in '79. Instead of looking it up I just went ahead and wrote the song. So '79 Granada is supposed to allude to the revolution in Granada, which actually happened in '81. I could have easily said '81 Granada, but I'm just lazy I guess.

Anyway, so the idea behind the song was to write a story that went so deep with the details that people would have no choice but to relate to my character and would then follow along and accept the points and the premise of my argument. First of all, it's a pretty simple story. If I'd just said the plot line of the story, it would be kind of corny and a cliché. A guy is raised by his mother, who is a prostitute, and a pimp kills her and in the end he gets revenge by killing the pimp.

And it's not clear why my character is picking up Jesus the pimp in the first place. It seems like we're just riding

I see

the red and white lights

as the ambulance flies

Reminds me of midnight in a dope fiend's
    eyes

And my nine-year-old self

as paramedics leave

Left

to bawl my eyes out on a neighbor's sleeve

To give illustrations

that are clear and clean

I'll take you two hours back

before this scene

Early in the morning

when the sun starts to creep

When the birds start to chirp

and crackheads go to sleep

Moms was comin' in

I heard her keys go clink

Wearin nothin but pumps

Bikini

and fake mink

Even though she served for fifty dollars a pop

Hardly had enough for rent

after Jesus re-copped

That day

the landlady got her rent

before he got his knot

Slammed momma's head

against the front bolt lock

Then

the pimp wit one arm

done harm

Reached back and plowed into her head like
    a farm

Never saw the act

locked in the back

I was cussin

Heard the blap-blap

of twenty head-crack percussion

and body blows

her body froze

from bolos to the spine

I was hysterically cryin

all she could do was whine

She didn't even have the strength

to say, "I love you, Boo"

But I said it to her

and

she knew that I knew

She was dead by the time the ambulance got
    on the case

But I never will forget

the plastic hand stuck in her face

Stop at the intersection

to ask Jesus bout directions

"Let's go to Frisco"

(I got very friendly vocal inflections)

Mob a left at MacArthur

to continue in flight


Me and Jesus the Pimp in a '79 Granada
    last night


Oakland do you wanna ride?

I can't hear you! Oakland do you wanna
    ride tonight? (2x)


The rain

dropped giant pearls

God was pissin on the world

or that old man who was snorin

rolled on over and earled

My temperature gauge read "cold and
    blistery"

Spinnin wheels

made each piece of asphalt history

This was Jesus debut

out the penitentiary

Fifteen years

but it seemed like a century

See

he went in the pen

for some other murder drama

Twelve years old

I wrote him

quote

I wanna be a pimp

comma

You accidentally killed my mom

no playa-hation points

You know how bitches act

shit

exclamation point

First

it was a set-up move

then

it was the truth

His letters were the only thing I had as
    a youth

But his lopsided game

See

was really counterfeit

So my little son Dominic

thinks that I'm a dick

Cause I was runnin round

like a little baby Jesus

To me

women had to be

Saints

Hos

or skeezers

And I don't think that it's gon end

til we make revolution

But who gon make the shit

if we worship prostitution?

Ain't no women finna die

for the same ol' conclusion

Put they life on the line

so some other pimp could use em

Pulled into a vacant lot

the road to recovery

around, but as it unfolds you realize, at the end at least, that I'm taking him to kill him. And at the same time, Jesus is supposed to represent the myth of Black capitalism. The '79 Granada, like I said, is the revolution, and we're taught that, just as my character is taught, that pimping or the philosophy that Jesus the pimp has is the "way out"—is the only way to be powerful. But the character comes to the conclusion that all of that is bullshit and it's hurt him in the past, through his mother, and it's turned him into a terrible person, and he gets rid of not only the sexist pimp ideology, but in a larger way, it's about the idea of Black folks being part of movements that have a class analysis as opposed to a bourgeois nationalist analysis. Anyway, I don't know if any of that comes through in the song, but that's what I wanted to do.

In the song I try to give the mother's character a voice by having her sing to the child, "You're just too beautiful for words." All of this I'm telling you is what my intent in writing this song was; however, as with many songs, the whole idea for it came with having a good first line: "Well he was smiling like a vulture as he rolled up the horticulture." That made me have to figure out, who was rolling up the horticulture, and who would be smiling like that? That was Jesus the pimp, and then it fell in with my earlier need to write a song about sexism.

It took me a while to write this song, as I knew that it would be a song that would be listened to many times. And I wanted to make it long, at that time I made many of my songs seven and eight minutes long, which is not good if you are trying to get it on the radio. In some ways, I was stubborn and that's what allowed me to make songs with a form such as this. In other ways, maybe it wasn't so good,

Left to right: Manuel Riley, Boots, Johnny Mitchell, Pointt Blank, E-Roc, and Khalid Wilson.

AUGUST 1

I don't know. Maybe The Coup would be more well known had I, you know, done things in the regular way.

Anyway, this is a song that I am very proud of, and I'm glad that other folks have name-checked it. Mac Mall wrote a song that was inspired by it. Monique Morris wrote a novel called *Too Beautiful for Words*, which was inspired by, based on, this song. I, however, kept the movie rights because I didn't and don't want this made into a movie. It's one of those things that, given a different person's political take on events, could be a really bad movie and racist story. So anyway, that's "Me and Jesus the Pimp in a '79 Granada Last Night." —BOOTS

RISBANE, CA ON THE SET OF THE "TAKIN' THESE" VIDEO. FRONT OF THE "MANSION" (MERCY HIGH SCHOOL). PHOTO TAKEN BY CARLA MATHIS.

## ME AND JESUS THE PIMP IN A '79 GRANADA LAST NIGHT
{CONTINUED}

Pulled out my pistol
as we brushed against the shrubbery
Jesus said
"Why the hell you pointin a gat?"
So I pulled a piece of game I could use
out the hat
I said
"This trip is over
we ain't finna ride on
This is for my mental
and my momma that I cried on
Microsoft muthafuckas
let bygones be bygones
but since I'm Macintosh
I'mma double click yo icon"
He struggled for life
then gave up the fight
Me and Jesus the Pimp in a '79 Granada
   last night

Oakland do you wanna ride?
I can't hear you! Oakland do you wanna ride
tonight? (2x)

137

## 20,000 GUN SALUTE

20,000 gun salute
get rowdy like you got a substitute
This slug's for Newt
shut your mouth
don't pollute
Army of down muthafuckas
shit
we tryin to recruit!

See now we're talkin
systematic
mack mechanics
decomposin
chosen
representatives
from the ho's been
known to act wit
pimp theatrics
a tactic necessary
In fact
they wanna have us buyin from the
    commissary
This commentary's
for my folks under involuntary
servitude
Cause bosses don't be servin you your
    monetary
Pervin you like rum'n'dairy
pulsin through your capillaries
Some inherit green
the rest just get our folks to bury
I'm abolitionary
wishin the judiciary
say this year for merry merry
"Free the penitentiary!"
Peoples gon rumble
as long as stomachs grumble
and crack pipes tumble
over asphalt that's crumbled
Hundreds come in bundles

and hop is mixed with funnels
Cause babies wit shoes too small gon
    stumble
This composition is sedition
opposition to the rulin class
Wishin
they get detonators hooked to their ignition
Keep my slacks creased
to punch the clock for the beast
As my rent don't cease
his pockets get obese
Can't have inner peace
without havin a piece
When the stepped on step up
we let the dragon release

20,000 gun salute
get rowdy like you got a substitute
This slug's for Newt
shut your mouth
don't pollute
Army of down muthafuckas
shit
we tryin to recruit!

Disaster!
The filthy rich bastards
wanna milk yo ass faster
ask fuh
no salvation comin from the damn pastor
Old ladies play canasta
under roofs of cracked plaster
Little kids dive in the trash for
discarded Dutchmasters
Dead patnahs on mural walls
Homeless kids takin baths up in gas
    station urinals
Shit the system can't cure at all
If everybody had a job
then stock value's sure to fall
Hundred million neck slashes
so these facists

can make sho that they check cashes
let's get masses
Wage struggle as direct classes
on just how we gonna
overthrow they bitch asses
give whiplashes
from the force as we make it tight
and ignite
the flames of takin over daily life
make it a right
to have food, threads and homestead
and Pac Bell won't ever cut your phone
    dead
we own it!
But these business
that love payin minimum wage
ain't gon let you take they shit
unless you showin a gauge
And if you do it by yourself
they gon' put you in a cage
If you in a rage
please meet me on the same page
with a

20,000 gun salute
get rowdy like you got a substitute
This slug's for Newt
shut your mouth
don't pollute
Army of down muthafuckas
shit
we tryin to recruit!

# BUSTERISMOLOGY

I'm risin like the vapors from the dank
Fuck the mirror in my pocket
had to break it for a shank
What you thank?
Walk the plank is my motherfuckin attitude
Right hand on the wheel
elbow out the window
leanin to the latitude
actin rude can get you blown up
torn up
But these teeny-boppers
ain't gon live to be a grown up
My muthafucka done got hisself into a spot
I got this nine
but it jam on every fifth shot
If we gon do this
we could this
but I'm trippin off
the factor that these bastards put me
    through this
Nuttin ass tricks
gangin up on my homie
Now I gots to do some shit
to leave yo kids lonely
The level of my life should be higher
Told E-Roc to jump in
and get up out the line of fire
Made a three-point turn
as the three joints burned
off they lips
actin hard
wit they face held firm
Calmly stated my acquaintance was no punk
You got a gat
I got a gat
now is you requestin funk?
They said no
E-Roc yelled, "Trick!"
When we start the revolution all they
    probably do is snitch

Chorus
When we start the revolution, all they
    probably do is snitch
When we start the revolution, all they
    probably do is snitch
When we start the revolution, all they,
    probably do is snitch! (2x)


I used to work at Mickey D's
And to my old buster-ass manager
licky these
Had me workin on hands and knees
scrubbin grease
And in the summer with the oven on
it's hundred-ten degrees
I would despise flippin fries
I guess his bitch-ass
thought he was the shit
with his little red and gold tie
I asked him why I couldn't get mo hours
He said it must be cause I lacked the
    mental powers
If I was smart
then I would be in his position
I left his nose
in a busted up condition
Only came back for my last check to pay
    me off
He told me then
that he wasn't gonna lay me off
Said I should quit
and it would be to my enjoyment
I fell for it and couldn't get my unemployment
To all the managers
on all the shifts
When we start this revolution
all y'all probably do is snitch!


Chorus (2x)

Now hella my folks
got respect for you, killa
Wit a raised black fist
and a pocket full of scrilla
Cap peelers want your autograph
say you know the path
But I do the math
my game bursts
like a bubble in the bath
Punk asses like you is just here for confusion
Be abusin rhetoric
and it's slightly amusin
You be cruisin all the networks
Ebony and Jet works
along with your efforts
now what's your net worth?
If you ain't talkin bout
endin exploitation
Then you just another
Sambo in syndication
Always sayin words
that's gon bring about elation
Never doin shit
that's gon bring us vindication
And while we gettin strangled by the
    slave-wage grippers
You wanna do the same
and say we should put you in business?
So you'll be next to the rulin class
lyin in a ditch
Cause when we start this revolution
all you probably do is snitch!

Chorus (2x)

# CARS AND SHOES

Now if you gettin in my car
don't sit down right away
Cause my passenger seat tilts sideways
And don't even try to lean the shit back
The whole damn thang'll fall off the track
Stick your hand out
and signal for a right
My window's stuck
plus I got a broken turn light
Naw I ain't dippin!
Sometimes I get a stuck brake
Got my rearview attached with some duct
tape
Keep yo knee right there!
I'm tryna keep that glove compartment
closed, player!
The seatbelt don't work
just tie it round your waist
If you crash through the window
just cover your face
The radio gets one station on AM
it's Chinese
but if you listen you could catch what they
sayin'
Stop complainin
I heard what you said
So what the seat spring poked you in the
leg?
Didn't know it stabbed you
but what you stompin' fo?
You finna put yo foot through that hole in
the floor!
Now what you say
you gonna sue me?
Awwww,
because the baby hurt his leg and got a
booby?
Now your feelings hurt
you wanna get up out my shit
Cool motherfucker
here you go
get yo' kicks

You need to act a little older!
If you want that door to open
you gon have to use yo shoulder
Get the fuck up out fool
you lose
why?
My car is better than yo shoes

Now if you get in my bucket baby, you gotta
sit on the flo
And I ain't go no license you know, I'm
tryin-a duck the po-po
Now if you get in my bucket baby, you gotta
sit on the flo
And I ain't go no license you know, I'm
tryin-a duck the po-po

See me in the town
you might think I'm a star
Every three months in a different car
Like the other day in a '81 Datsun
with my alternator rollin shotgun
Or in the fall
in a '88 Seville
Pushin it wit my foot down the hill
Once I did a job
the lady didn't wanna pay me
So she offered me a hooptie instead
I said maybe
Cause it looked like it went through a war
Missin a door
three out of four
Ain't bad
but is it safe to drive?
I'll wait til payday
then make it live
Fixed the beat first cause that's my choice
A bucket with the beat look like a Rolls
Royce!
Next week it broke down on the Bay Bridge
And lemme tell you
that motherfucker dangerous!
Had a hundred so I hit the auction block off
Got a seven-six Pinto

with some knockoffs
Catchin buses be gettin me to work late
And you know that slow down my pay rate
Down to zero
No alignment make it kinda hard to steer
though
They need to pay me for all these adven-
tures
Tell em to my grandkids when I got
dentures
Makin a buck really costs a buck fiddy
It's only that cheap if your car's shitty
Muthafuckas laughin but it beats the AC
transit blues
Shit
my car is better than my shoes

Now if you get in my bucket baby, you gotta
sit on the flo
And I ain't go no license you know, I'm
tryin-a duck the po-po
Now if you get in my bucket baby, you gotta
sit on the flo
And I ain't go no license you know, I'm
tryin-a duck the po-po

# BREATHING APPARATUS

Shit
I give a fuck who did the killing
Got a puncture in my lung
tell em gimme penicillin
Fingertips ain't got no feelin
pain-killin
gimme codeine
Don't let me vomit up my guts
let's keep the flo clean
I seen em comin for a mile through the rearview
I'll tell you one thing bout them po-pos
they don't love you

Lean over the bed and let me whisper close
Watch these muthafuckas with the stethoscopes
You know I'm uninsured up in this b-i-otch
My medical plan
was to not get shot
I get the—

"One two breathe!" "Code blue!"
"Two two breathe! "Code blue!
*bzzzzzzzzzzzzt* "Clear!"
*bzzzzzzzzzzzzt*
"I've got a pulse!"

Nurse, what's the status?
E please don't let em fuck with my breathing
apparatus

I ain't gon let em fuck with your breathing
apparatus
Please don't let em fuck with my breathing
apparatus
I ain't gon let em fuck with your breathing
apparatus
Please don't let em fuck with my breathing
apparatus

I'm feelin hostile
with this fuckin hose up my nostril

My bills be colossal
creditors be followin me
like apostles
I jostle the fossils
of thoughts that's given
Fuck these motherfuckers tryin to pimp me
for livin
Scrape up scrilla for the box I'm in
if we can't hock some ends
for this oxygen

Ay man I got a disease
It's called broke, with no motherfuckin respect
and it's a STD, but you ain't never gon nut
cause it come from a long legacy of gettin fucked

Aight, hook it up

I ain't gon let em fuck with your breathing
apparatus
Please don't let em fuck with my breathing
apparatus (2x)

See I'm a communist
I'll tell yo mama the truth
And now they wanna assassinate me
like they John Wilkes Booth
But umm
recognize sperm
cause yo brain is the maternity
Conception through yo ear
now my game lasts through
eterni-*cough*-ty
*cough, cough*

"Breathe again, breathe again . . ."
And I will never breathe again . . ."

[Doctor]
Well, I've been looking at the patient's stats
It seems as if he's lost his will to pay

# THE REPO MAN SINGS FOR YOU

It's the Repo Man
Reposession is my occupation
It's not my fault you facin
Foreclosure
I told ya
I'm just an agent
workin for the man
and his manuscript say you owe him for this
land
Don't cry to me
and don't lie to me
Actin like you ain't home
fakin on the phone
You shoulda thought about that when you
bought the Benzy
You missed a few increments
now we gotta come and get yo shit
If you slip
on the payments
I get paid
to make sure that you pay rent
or get out
throw all your clothes in the streets
Frozen meats
out your refrigerator
then my boys come back and get it later
with the forklift
we don't care how hard you worked
we takin yo shit
It's too late
your payment's way past your due date
You couldn't hide from me
even with a new face
or plastic surgery
your debt's outstandin
I don't care about your family
don't hand me
no excuses
you know it's useless
no one's stoppin me
Just get off the property before I bring the cops

with me
Possibly
this could turn into a criminal act
Gimme your fax machine
PlayStation in the basement
Adjacent to the big-screen television
You can't tell the system no
we gotta get the dough
The company want they Gs
or the keys
to the convertible
and hey
nothin personal
okay?
I'm just doin my job
Collectin on your debts
now you're losin a wad
Bruisin your wallet
whatever in your pocketbook
all get took
to my agency
then they payin me
It ain't fazin me
that's my thing
When I mob off with yo shit
listen to me sing

La la la la la la la la, la la la la la (8x)

thck!
One, paycheck from sleepin on the street
tchka!
Two/too, many bills my scrill don't meet
tchka!
Three-day notice from the landlord on the seat
Fo-fo
caliber shots ain't discrete
But motherfuckers still jack frequent
no secret
cause they shit be delinquent
And on closer inspection
reposession collection
motivates birth protection in the brokest

section
In other words
the ghetto
Repo Man
pullin strings like Geppetto
Squeeze two at him
let go
Cause I just gotta be real
I'm tired of informercials
with them five-year payment deals
See
I was sleepin on the carpet
in my apartment
when I heard my car ignition
cause somebody sparked it
So I run all the way
down the hallway
full throttle
Don't give in is my motto
so I bust him with a bottle
He screamin
"Whatchu gon' pay me with?"
Then he started laughin
singin
crazy shit

La la la la la la la, la la la la la

I said,
"SHUT THE FUCK UP"
and then I banked him in the jaw
But that was no use
even though he skedaddled
bill collectors make my phone rattle
tell my kids don't tattle
When you pick up the receiver
I'm sick with a fever
You don't know where I am either
Even hillbillies at a party line dancin
get they Ford trucks with poor financing
Banks that give the loan figure
"Damn
in the worst case

we makin money cause
we had it in the first place!"
And where was it
that they got that cash from?
You when you deposit it from bustin yo ass
Well two weeks after
that last altercation
I noticed my front lock
had a slight alteration
My TV was gone
and out the window from my room
I heard the Repo Man sing his devious tune
it went

La la la la la la la, la la la la la (8x)

# STEAL THIS ALBUM

## U.C.P.A.S.

BOOTS RILEY

### U.C.P.A.S.

Undas, Cops, Pigs and Shit
They be gettin on my nerves
I'm bout to have a fit
I need land
a place where no money is spent
I'll kick back
and live life immaculate

Undas, Cops, Pigs and Shit
They be gettin on my nerves
I'm bout to have a fit
I need land
a place where no money is spent
I'll kick back
and live life immaculate

Now if this party was a class
I'd be a teacher
It's F.T.S. and The Coup
a double feature
Now if this party was a car
I'd be the driver
I'm rappin third
the mic is smellin like saliva
The emperor
that muthafucka's
ass naked
We'll take you higher
than when you had your last dank hit
It's not surprisin

www.illcrew.com/thecoup

that when folks start to uprisin

there's police on the horizon

they been there all along

they just good at they disguising

the po-pos

supposed to keep the peace?

they gotta make the bosses money

increase

You never seen the police

break up a strike

by hittin the boss

with his baton pipe

And you ain't never gon see one

but when we take over

it's gon' be poppin

like Re-Run

Boots from The Coup

lightin the dark like a toker

Much love to my folkers

all aces and jokers

Undas, Cops, Pigs and Shit

They be gettin on my nerves

I'm bout to have a fit

I need land

a place where no money is spent

I'll kick back

and live life immaculate

# UNDER-DOGS

"Underdogs," was one of the first songs that was emotionally real to me. That I was emotionally able to let down my guard and just write what I felt. Doing this song, and having it work, actually allowed me to write later songs like "Wear Clean Draws," "Nowalaters," "Ijustwannala-yaroundalldayinbedwithyou," and "Laugh/Love/Fuck." They may not seem related, but I wrote this song and just let my feelings go and trusted that my ideas would come out more organically.

The song started as a letter to a friend of mine who had really broken my trust. He was somebody that I had tried to help out a lot and that my father had tried to help out a lot, and I found out about some lies that he had told to get over on like a really small amount of money from me and from my father. And it really hurt me, but thinking about that song and writing that song turned into writing about

## UNDERDOGS

This is for my folkers who got bills overdue
This is for my folkers
um, check one two
This is for my folkers
never lived like a hog
Me and you
toe to toe
I got love for the underdog

This is for my folkers who got bills overdue
This is for my folkers
um, check one two
This is for my folkers
never lived like a hog
Me and you
toe to toe
I got love for the underdog

I raise this glass
for the ones who die meaninglessly
And the newborns who get fed intravenously
Somebody's mama
caught a job
and a welfare fraud case
When she breathe
she swear it feel like
plastic wrap around her face
Lights turned off
and this the third month the rent is late
Thoughts of bein homeless
cryin til you hyperventilate
Despair
permeates the air
and sets in your hair
The kids
play with that one toy
they learned how to share
Comin home don't never seem
to be a celebration
Bills stay piled up on the coffee table
like they decoration
Heapin spoons of peanut butter
big ass glass of water
Make the hunger subside
save the real food for your daughter

THE COUP - UNDERDOGS (LIVE)
South Paw, Brooklyn, NY
10/30/05

From a video shot by Vince Tocce.

STEAL THIS ALBUM (1998)

the position he was in and expanding on that.

And relating it to the position that I was in at the time, because a lot of that stuff that I throw in there is really just examples of what I've gone through. And some of the things are specific examples of what this particular friend had gone through too.

The way that I perform the song has a slightly different take than the way that it was written. As written, the last line is "They'd tear this motherfucker up if they really loved you," and then it goes straight to the chorus: "This is for my folkers who got bills overdue." Alright.

But when I recorded the song I said, "They'd tear this motherfucker up if they really loved you, and so would you." So it's kind of an invitation, a challenge to the listener, saying that making a change to the system is part of loving yourself. It's also personally the part of the song that's connected to how I started writing the song in the first place. Because this particular person had used certain campaigns and certain things that were happening in the community as a reason to get over and get himself paid. He wasn't stealing from anybody except for me and my father, but he was using some of those things to get over on us. And the reality is that this was a really smart dude and I felt like part of the reason he was doing this was because he didn't love himself.

And that may sound real wishy-washy and hippie, but I just know specifically that this person had no faith in himself, no faith in the idea that he could join together with others and change things. So he used some of his politics to get over on others for himself. I don't know if I'm being clear because if you don't know the situation, you might not understand it. Anyway, the point is that this

BOOTS RILEY

# E P

# Revolution
# hip-hop sty

*Oakland's Young Comrades*
*oriented culture with politi*
## By Christian Parenti

NIGHT IS FALLING on the sprawling Fre section of Oakland. The streets are plac inside an innocuous storefront office lution is brewing. Not the hyper historical-reenactment, "buy-my-comm newspaper-now" sort, or the military-fantasy "cap- now" sort, but a new, pragmatic, and impeccably hip b revolution.

Welcome to the headquarters of the Young Comra crew of black activists in their late teens and 20s. lounge end of the split-level space, a black-owned, Oa based cable station flickers away silently. In the back, up steps, one section of the office resembles a control boot three desks, a table, a bookshelf, two fax machines, funky old word processor.

"This is just some stuff we rolled up in an ad hoc way," says Raymond Riely, a.k.a. Boots, gesturing to the clean, well-organized office. Boots, one of the Young Comrades' core members, also performs with the Coup, a hip-hop group of national fame that has released two bumping, highly political albums. "The Young Comrades are a revolutionary organization, but we don't want to take ourselves away from what are technically reform struggles. People have to see revolutionary change as practical; it's got

monologues can be he KALX's *Amandla Show* a Radio Berkeley. Like mos Comrades members, Jame his politics with a heavy dos ture.

## Organizing with cul
Among the group's cultu organizing strategies is the getting a tape press to pr weekly audio publication t tures news, analysis, and n wrapped up in hip-hop for nancial hurdles have kept th

## UNDERDOGS
{CONTINUED}

You feel like swingin haymakers
at a moving truck
You feel like laughing
so it seems like you don't give a fuck
You feel like getting so high
You'll smoke the whole damn crop
You feel like cryin
but you think that you might never stop
Homes with no heat
stiffen your joints like arthritis
If this was fiction
it'd be easier to write this
Some folks try to front
like they so above you
They'd tear this motherfucker up if they really loved you
And so would you

This is for my folkers who got bills overdue
This is for my folkers
um, check one two
This is for my folkers
never lived like a hog
Me and you
toe to toe
I got love for the underdog
This is for my folkers who got bills overdue
This is for my folkers
um, check one two
This is for my folkers
never lived like a hog
Me and you
toe to toe
I got love for the underdog

There's certain tricks of the trade
to try and hault your defeat
Like taking tupperware to an "all you can eat"
Returning used shit for new
sayin you lost your receipt

And writin four-figure checks
when your accounts deplete
Then all your problems pile up
about a mile up
Thinkin about a partner you can dial up
to help you out this vile stuff
Whole family sleepin on the futon
while you clippin coupons
Eatin salad
tryin to get full off the croutons
Crosstown
the situation is identical
Somebody gettin strangled
by the system and its tentacles
Misconceptions raise questions to be solved
A lot of dope boys is broke
a lot of homeless got jobs
You can make eight bones an hour
til you pass out
and still be ass out
Most pyramid schemes
don't let you cash out
They say this generation
made the harmony break
But crime rise consistent
with the poverty rate
You take the workers from jobs
you gon have murders in mobs
A gang of preachers screamin sermons
over murmurs and sobs
Sayin "Pray for a change from the Lord above you"
They'd tear this motherfucker up if they really loved you
And so would you

This is for my folkers who got bills overdue
This is for my folkers
um, check one two
This is for my folkers
never lived like a hog
Me and you
toe to toe
I got love for the underdog

Article about the Young Comrades in the *East Bay Express*. Circa '96.

song came from a really personal place, but I tried to connect it to things that were going on in the world and it's one of my favorite songs.

Usually people ask me what are some of my favorite songs that I've written and it's hard for me to pick, but, and I always forget this one, when I'm saying it I realize it's one of my favorite songs. That's "Underdogs."

I'd also like to say that a lot of my language was really connected to the ways people speak in the Bay Area, which are, you know, are becoming wider known, but a lot of plays on words or puns that I used were based on Bay Area slang and sometimes went over folks' heads.

I really couldn't think about that while writing most of my songs. It was just too much to have to answer to, but anyway, I think some of that is in here, in some of the recorded version of it. I think, you know, at first in the recorded version I say "D boys" instead of "dope boys," but live now I realize that just for people to understand I say "dope boys" because "D boys" meant folks that were selling dope, and a lot of people heard that and they didn't understand, they thought I was saying "B boys," you know on some sort of hip-hop thing, like we're saying that dancers are broke. I say, "A lot of D boys is broke, a lot of homeless got jobs." Now when I do it live I say, "A lot of dope boys is broke, a lot of homeless got jobs." — BOOTS

# UNDERDOGS
{CONTINUED}

This is for my folkers who got bills overdue
This is for my folkers
um, check one two
This is for my folkers
never lived like a hog
Me and you
toe to toe
I got love for the underdog

You like this song cause it's relatable
it's you in a rhyme
We go to stores
that only let us in two at a time
We live in places
where it costs to get your check cashed
Arguments about money
usually drown out the tec blasts
Work six days a week
can't sleep Saturdays though
Muscles tremblin
like a pager when the battery's low
And you just don't know
where the years went
Although
every long shift feels like a year spent
And you can write your resume
but it wouldn't even mention
All the life lessons learned
during six years of detention
Or how you learned the police
was just some handicappers
On the ground
next to broken glass and candy wrappers
So don't accept
my collects on the phone
Just hit me at the house
so I know I ain't alone
And we can chop it up

about this messed up system
Homies that's been killed
how we always gon miss em
It's almost impossible
survivin on this fraction
Sip a 40 to the brain
for the chemical reaction
You gotta hustle
cause they tryin to push and shove you
I'll tear this motherfucker up since I really love you
And so would you

This is for my folkers who got bills overdue
This is for my folkers
um, check one two
This is for my folkers
never lived like a hog
Me and you
toe to toe
I got love for the underdog
This is for my folkers who got bills overdue
This is for my folkers
um, check one two
This is for my folkers
never lived like a hog
Me and you
toe to toe
I got love for the underdog

# SNEAKIN' IN

Photo from the *East Bay Express*. Circa '96.

**ng out:** *Young Comrades members Reginald Brown, left, and Raymond Riely, a.k.a. Boots, talk with Sharon Baptiste of Hayward at registration table behind the Durant Square Flea Market in East Oakland.*

## SNEAKIN' IN

Now
I calculate the beatin
for approximated speakin
Play it at your party
for intoxicated freakin
One
for the muthafuckas at the party
Two
for the DJs bumpin this for me
Three
for the girls with the fake ID
and a pound
if you snuck through the back for free
See
sneakin into shit
probably always been my hobby
1985 in the Henry J. lobby
Ten bones
for the Fresh Fest
to me was like robbery
Tennis shoes squeakin
security tried to mob me
People screamin so loud
they lungs got broke when
Short grabbed the mic
and started yellin out "Oakland!"
Not the type of brother
that's hard with a death wish
but one thing that I'll die for
is bein on the guest list
I'm talkin bout a pissyfit
sayin loud explicit shit
"Can't you read my name muthafucka?
    Ain't you literate?!"
I be sayin this
even if it ain't legitimate
Although it ain't considerate
I get in with no scrilla spent

Caught the 57 bus
to the Coliseum
Run-D.M.C. and LL
gotta see em
Negotiatin with a guard
out by the trailer
Me and twenty patnahs
got in for a Taylor
Later in the game
shit was much more elaborate
Muthafuckas rocked the spot
with fake laminates
Show em to security
and it was like BAM!
On stage with Ice Cube at the Summer Jam
I'm not a fronter and
this ain't no cover band
I'm always givin you the really
and no other than
Alameda Drive-In
didn't wanna pay a buck
Five muthafuckas
layin flat in a mini-truck
Used to sneak in
to the Eastmont Cinemas
Through the exit
sometimes about ten of us
But you know
I guess it was so easy
cause they playin movies that's already on TV
Most of them flicks
I can't recommend
But back then
half the fun was sneakin in
See me in the alley
but
nah
I ain't no crack ho
I'm waitin for my folks
to open up the back do'

# PISS ON YOUR GRAVE

PISS ON YOUR GRAVE

*Chorus*

Uhhhh!!
I wanna piss on your grave!
make me feel alright!
Yaa Yaa Yaa!! (2x)

While you was eatin'
T-bone steaks
in palatial estates,
ornate with gates that automate
so those you hate could only spectate,
I was kissing my mate
through iron grates
while the guards wait,
50 cent rate for making license plates
My Papermate pen shakes
vibrates from 808 quakes
over breaks
dug outta crates
that sag from weight
of the vinyl plates
girls work till their back aches
and their breasts can't lactate
you're laughin' to the bank

"Photo with some folks whose names I forget. Obviously, Pam and E-Roc on either side of me. The late Bay Area legend Cougnut kneeling, and Dawud—of *Steal This Album* and *Pick a Bigger Weapon* skit fame—to the right behind Pam. Sacramento, 1995." —BOOTS

smilin', showin' all your plaque flakes
contesting, contesting 1, 2, 3
never shoulda been put in the penitentiary
Boots from The Coup would like to say
I'll shove these foodstamps down your throat
just to block your airway
and that's the fair way
cuz everyday
you're on a moola mission
military killin' millions til you low on ammunition
bodies beyond recognition
twisted complex positions
then their kids work in your factories
and die of malnutrition
see your net profit stats
hold some murderous facts
but if you listen to the news
you mighta
heard it was blacks
you got us herded in shacks
I got the pertinent tax
How 'bout the one for when I bust my ass
and you relax
I'll hit your head wit an axe
play soccer with your brain
to make it official
slice your jugular vein
still writin songs
that my momma could sing
and if you feel some yellow drips on your
skull
it ain't rain

Chorus

That bitch ass on the front of a buck
never gave a fuck
he forced his black women slaves
to give him dick sucks
and when he bust a nut
he'd laugh and cackle

let the leather whip crackle
send 'em back to pick tobacco
shackled
wouldn't give 'em nil
so his homies stacked bills
fought on flatland and hill
to keep the British out the till, scrill
kept Washington dumpin em in ditches
so slave owning son of a bitches
could keep their riches
which is how the war got funded
with two centuries of juice
from black slaves' bodies
and the profits they produced
you could deduce
that these men might win
fit right in
and make rights then
just for rich white men
so they quit fightin
and wrote up a declaration
protective decoration
for their business operations
a gorilla pimpin' nation
no freedom
just savage
now the whole world's ravaged
from their hunger for the cabbage
Your fifth-period history teacher's
tellin lies like a tweeker
bump this song through the speaker
watch their face get weaker
less they righteous
and they kickin the facts
they gon smile
cuz this shit is on wax
one thing I gots to ask
George Washington
down in hell
can you see me?
I'm standin on your grave
and I'm finsta take a pee-pee

Chorus
Knock knock muthafucka, yes once again
I'll make you pay for your sins
in the trunk o' your Benz
see you's an always fitted
always acquitted
parasitic leech
cain't be burned off my back
wit' no fiery speech
your hands is soft as a peach
cuz you ain't never did work
been rich ever since
your daddy's dick went squirt
have you ever hurt from your back?
ducked from rat-a-tat-tats?
seen your mama on crack?
lived in a Pontiac?
drank baby Similac
so you could have protein?
(just for enough energy
to hustle up some mo' green?)
I could paint some mo' scenes
vergin' on the obscene
but I'd rather show up at your palace
with a mob scene
I spoke to my accountant
who spoke to my attorney
who counseled my financial advisor
on a gurney
it's about fifty dollars
and that's almost like a sale
cuz it costs too damn much
to let your rich ass inhale
true liberation ain't no word in the head
I'm yellin' murder 'em dead
for some fish, steak and bread
you pay me 10 Gs a year,
I pay you fifteen million hun'ed?
Sorry, you just ain't in the budget

Chorus

# FIXATION

"Fixation" was one of the quickest songs I wrote; I wrote it in ten minutes. **My friend Keith McArthur actually made the beat on this; it was originally for a compilation. He had a beat and I needed some money and at the time there were a lot of rappers getting a lot of credit for their supposed skill in rapping—what it came down to was technically they rap the same suffix over and over for four to eight lines. So, I always was real vocal in my critique of this being the reason that someone is called "skilled."**

**A bunch of folks got famous from that. And you know, it just seemed like a gimmick to me, so I needed to write a song and I decided to use that gimmick while talking about the fact that that was a gimmick and talking about the fact that many of the folks that did that weren't talking about anything much in their song.**

**To talk about and then to also make some of my statements about the way I think society works. Anyway, that's "Fixation."** — BOOTS

# FIXATION

well
this is verbal penetration
alert your school administration
if you act like a dick
castration
it just brings me elation
your misleading presentation
was just boring oration
gunclaps
from my TEC will be your standing ovation
beat-per-minute calculations
match aorta palpitations
which speed up if you eat that greasy defecation
at Nation's
tear along the perforation
means collection notification
and you know I stack my scrilla
in negative denominations
and thats a damn abomination
it takes all my concentration
to not rob armored transportation
and collect compensation
but it takes
contemplation
conspiration
conversation
and propagation
information dissemination
and tribulations
no hesitation
indoctrination
affiliation,
penitentary and jail evasion
for liberation
and publications
spell THE COUP with capitalizations

I was on the verge of ejaculation
police performed a home invasion
so I cut off the illumination
and jumped up out the ventilation
they were in anticipation
waiting in Voltron formation
I performed circumnavigation
and then crawled through the foliation
started my legs to gyration
caught me
took me to the station
valuables confiscation
started the interrogation
wanted to know about this organization
causing business complications
said they wanted pacification
I said "I know all yo machinations!"
but you want mo exploitation
you gets no respect
no information
one mo thing for your gestation
I think you should try self-fornication!

# GENOCIDE AND JUICE (1994)

1. FAT CATS, BIGGA FISH
2. PIMPS (FREE STYLIN' AT THE FORTUNE 500 CLUB)
3. TAKIN' THESE
4. GUNSMOKE
5. THE NAME GAME
6. SANTA RITA WEEKEND
7. REPO MAN
8. INTERROGATION

# FAT CATS, BIGGA FISH

Okay, so "Fat Cats, Bigga Fish" was actually a song that I wrote to help me deal with a problem. I'd written this song, "Pimps: Freestylin' at the Fortune 500 Club," because it had the chance of being on the *Menace II Society* soundtrack. I wanted to write a song with the title "Pimps," but make it be about this stuff that I talk about, and so that's how the song "Pimps" came about. "Pimps" starts out in this high-class party with Fortune 500 club CEOs and businessmen, and a Rockefeller is there, a Getty is there, and I'm like, okay, I want a song that shows how we get here, how we get to this party. So I worked backwards from there. How would the listener get to this party, what's the connection between the street and this party? And so that led me how we get to this party because we're following a butler, a waiter who's working at the party. The protagonist of the story is a waiter and he's listening to all these things, and maybe he's pickpocketing, well whoa whoa whoa whoa, how does this guy keep his job if he does that? So, maybe he's not really a waiter, maybe he snuck in there, and maybe he has a whole life and an idea about the world that has led him here. And what would his reactions be at this party?

So "Fat Cats, Bigga Fish" ends up being about a small-time pickpocket who has developed an idea and almost an ideology about hustling and how it empowers him. That ideology makes him have this false feeling that he is able to manipulate the world to his liking. And in reality this is a small-time hustler who has to try to get free food by lying to a girl at a burger shop, and you know, who has a stolen bus pass and things like that. I know a lot of people like this, or I knew a lot of people at the time, I still know some, I think, but anyway . . . so what he learns after he sneaks into the party using his cousin's tux is that, you know, there are hustlers in the world so big, so powerful that he could never hope to be on their level, and that the whole system is one big hustle. That story ends there and begins with "Pimps."

In "Fat Cats, Bigga Fish," I wanted to deal with also the gentrification that was happening in Oakland and that happened all over the world and why it happens—why police brutality and prison population and arrest figures go up when they are trying to gentrify an area, so I deal with some of those things. — BOOTS

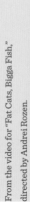

From the video for "Fat Cats, Bigga Fish," directed by Andrei Rozen.

"THERE ARE HUSTLERS IN THE WORLD SO BIG, SO POWERFUL THAT HE COULD NEVER HOPE TO BE ON THEIR LEVEL."

GENOCIDE AND JUICE (1994)

# FAT CATS, BIGGA FISH

c-c-c-come with it
get down get down get down
c-c-c-come with it
get down get down get down

It's
almost ten o'clock see
I got a ball of lint for property
so I slip my beenie on sloppily
and promenade out to take up a collection
I got game like I read the directions
I'm wishin that I had an automobile
as I feel the cold wind rush past
but let me state
that I'm a hustler for real
so you know I got the stolen bus pass

just as
the bus pulls up and I step to the rear
this ole lady look like she drank a forty of
fear
I see my ole school partnah said his
brother got popped
pay my respects
"Can you ring the bell?"
(we came to my stop)

the street light reflects
off the piss on the ground
which reflects off the hamburger sign that
    turns round
which reflects off the chrome of the BMW
which reflects off the fact that I'm broke
now what the fuck is new?

I need loot
I spot the muthafucka in the tweed suit
I'm in his ass quicker than a kick from a
    greased boot
eased up
slow and discreet
could tell he was suspicious by the way
    he slid his feet

didn't wanna fuck up
the come up
so I
smiled
winked my eye
said "Hey, how it's hanging guy?"
bumped into his shoulder
but he passed with no reaction
damn this muthafucka had a hella of
Andrew Jacksons

I'm a thief
a pickpocket
give a fuck what you call it
used to call em fat cats
i just call em wallets
getting federal
aint just a klepto
master card or visa
I gladly accept those
sneaky muthafucka with a scam
know how to pull it
got a mirror in my pocket
but that wont stop no bullets
story just begun
but you already know
aint no need to get down
shit
I'm already low

c-c-c-come with it
get down get down get down
c-c-c-come with it
get down get down get down

My footsteps echo in the darkness
my teeth clench tight like a fist in the
    cold sharp mist
I look down
and I hear my stomach growlin
step to burger king to attack it like a
    shaolin
I never pay for shit that I can get by
doing dirt
Linger to the girl cashier

and start to flirt
all up in her face
and her breath was like murder
damn the shit i do for a free hamburger

"Well
you got my number
you gon call me tonite?"
"It depends
is them burgers attached to a price?
Im just kidding
I'mma call
even write you love letters
thanks for the burgers
Um
hook me up with a Dr. Pepper?"
"That's cool
you want some ice?"
"Yeah
and some fries would be hella nice"
"My managers coming
Play it off okay?
Have a nice day!"
I'm up outta here anyway

I use peoples
before they use me
cuz you could get got by a Uzi over an OZ
that's what a OG told me
gots to find someplace warm and cozy
to eat the vittles that I just got
came to an underground parking lot
this place is good as any
fuck its all good
walked in
found a car
hopped and sat up on the hood
Ate my burger
threw back my cola
somebody said "Hey!"
it was a rent-a-pig
I thought it was a roller
"Want me to call the cops?"
I dont want them to see me
Looked down

Saw that I was sitting on a Lamborghini

It was Rollses
Ferraris
and Jags by the dozen
A building door opened
Damn
it was my cousin
getting off of work
dressed up
no lie
tux
cummerbund
and a black bow tie
I was like "Hey!"
"Who is it?"
"Me."
"Oh
what's up, man.
I just quit this company
they hella racist and the pay was too low"
I said "Riiight.
What was up in there though?"
"A party with rich muthafuckas
I don't know the situation
I know they got cabbage
owning corporations
IBM
Chrysler
and shit is what they said"
Just then a light bulb went off in my head

they be thinking all black folks is
    resembling
give me your tux and I'll do some pocket
swindling
finna change in the bathroom
and not freeze off my nuts
lets take a short break
while i get into this tux

aight
i'm ready

c-c-c-come with it

get down get down get down
c-c-c-come with it
get down get down get down

Fresh dressed
like a million bucks
I be the flyest muthafucka in a afro and a
tux
my arm is at a right angle up
silver tray in my hand
"May I interest you in some caviar ma'am"
my eyes shoots round the room
there and here
noticing the diamonds in the chandelier
background: Barry Manilow
Copacabana
and a strong-ass scent of stogies from
Havana

wasn't no place where a brother might been
snobby ole ladies drinking champagne
with rich white men
alright then
lets begin this
nights like this is good for business
five minutes in the mix noticed several
different cliques
talking
giggling and shit
with one muthafucka in betwixt
and everbody else jocking him
throttling
found out later he owned Coca-Cola Bottling
talking to a black man
Who's he?
Confused me
looking hella bourgie
ass all tight and sedity
recognized him
as the mayor of my city
who treats young black men like Frank
Nitty

Mr. Coke said to Mr. Mayor
"You know we got a process

like Ice T's hair
we put up the funds for your election
    campaign
and oh
um
waiter can you bring the champagne?
Our real estate firm
says opportunities arousing
to make some condos out of low income
    housing

immediately
we need some media heat
to say that gangs run the street
and then we bring in the police fleet
harass and beat everybody till they look
    inebriated
when we buy the land muthafuckas will
    appreciate it
Don't worry about the Urban League or
    Jesse Jackson
my man that owns Marlboro
donated a fat sum?

That's when I stepped back some
to contemplate what few know
sat down
wrestled with my thoughts like a sumo
aint no one player
that could beat this lunacy
aint no hustler on the street
could do a whole community
this is how deep shit can get
it reads macaroni on my birth certificate
puddintang is my middle name
but I cant hang
I'm getting hustled
only knowing half the game

# PIMPS (FREE STYLIN' AT THE FORTUNE 500 CLUB)

Now "Pimps" is basically about the people I mentioned before, they're at this party in "Fat Cats, Bigga Fish." **John Paul Getty and J. D. Rockefeller—I think it's J. D. Rockefeller, anyway one of the Rockefellers—are talking at a party and they figured out this trick to do with their voices to sound like authentic rappers and they're trying it out at the party, and quickly the actors' voices we have on the recording playing Rockefellers and the Gettys are able to turn into my and E-Roc's voices. Trump is on there too, on the original version, but right here is my verse. So that's what that is, and "Pimps" ends with the People breaking in and busting up the party.**

**And this image goes into "Taking These," in which the chorus is "we are takin' these if you please, we are takin' these if you don't please," which was inspired by the Disney movie with the Siamese cats—*Lady and the Tramp*, I think. And there are these Siamese cats saying, "we are Siamese if you please." — BOOTS**

# PIMPS (FREE STYLIN' AT THE FORTUNE 500 CLUB)

Well if you're blind as Helen Keller
You could see I'm David Rockefeller
So much cash
up in my bathroom is a ready-teller
I'm outrageous
I work in stages
like syphilis
But no need for prophylactics
I'mma up you on some mean old mack shit
Ain't buff
but my green gots amino acid
Keep my hoes in check
no rebellions
if yo ass occur
Shit
it wouldn't be the first time
I done made a massacre
Nigga please
how you figure these
Muthafuckas like me
got stocks
bonds
and securities
No impurities
straight Anglo-Saxon
When my family got they sex on
Don't let me get my flex on
Do some gangsta shit
make the army go to war for Exxon
Long as the money flow
I'll be makin dough
Welcome to my little pimp school
How you gon' beat me at this game?
I made the rules
Flash a little cash
make you think you got class
But you're really sellin ass
and hoe
keep off my grass
Less you're cuttin it
See
I'm runnin shit
Trick
all y'all muthafuckas is simps
I'm just a pimp

"Back then, in the 90s, DJ pools were important. This was the way you got your music played by party DJs. This was the 'The Pros' DJ pool report. DJs belonged to the pool, and got records given to them." — BOOTS

**GENOCIDE AND JUICE (1994)**

**165**

## THE PROS REPORT

PROFESSIONAL DISCO PROGRAMMERS ASSOC. — THE PROS

440 GRAND AVENUE  GROUND FLOOR
OAKLAND  CALIFORNIA  94610-5029
Office 510/839-3000  Fax 510/839-3201

SINCE 1979   15th ANNIVERSARY   100 MEMBERS

DECEMBER 15 1994 — Season's Greetings

LAST CHART OF 1994
NEXT CHART: JANUARY 15, 1995

### JAMMIN' LP CUTS

ALL ALONE ● SLICK RICK
CUZ IT'S WRONG ● SLICK RICK
TAKE 'EM UNDER ● FLATLINERS
BODYAHEAD ● REDMAN
IN THE HOUSE ● PETE ROCK
INDDLOVE ● H-TOWN
WHATCHA SEE ● PARIS
ALLADAT ● BRAND NUBIAN
IN FRONT OF THE KIDS ● EXTRA PROLIFIC
4-PLAY ● Y? N-VEE
STR8 HUSTLER ● Y? N-VEE
GOTTA GET TO KNOW ME ● CASSERINE

### TEN SUPER PICKS

I'M GOING DOWN ● Y? N-VEE
EAST COAST/WEST COAST ● SIMPLE E
DE ABYSS ● SIMPLE E
IT'S A STREET FIGHT ● B.U.M.S.
I LIKE WHAT YOU'RE DOING TO ME ● JOYA
NUTHIN' BUT A TRAMP ● GOLDY
I AIN'T NO LADY ● H.W.A.
SLYDE ● CAMEO
BORN TO LIVE ● O.C.
DEDICATION TO BAMBAATAA ● JUSTICE SYSTEM

*** HAS EITHER VISITED OR WAS PRESENTED US WITH A GOLD/PLATINUM

### Reggae DanceHall

| 100 | LC | TITLE | ARTIST | LABEL |
|---|---|---|---|---|
| 1 | 5 | YAGA YAGA | TERROR FABULOUS*** | EAST WEST |
| 2 | 7 | SOUTH CENTRAL | SUPER CAT | COLUMBIA |
| 3 | 3 | INKA | VICIOUS | EPIC |
| 4 | 6 | BOOTS TRAP | STEELE PULSE | MCA |
| 5 | 2 | BREATHE AGAIN | SWEET-TEA | RELATIVITY |
| 6 | 8 | BACK TO MY ROOTS | STEELE PULSE | MCA |
| 7 | 4 | KING OF KINGS | TERRY GANZIE | PROFILE |
| 8 | 6 | SWEET HONEY | BORN JAMERICANS*** | DELICIOUS VINYL |
| 9 | 1 | TAKE IT EASY | MAD LION | WEEDED |
| 10 | 10 | CALL ME SISTER CAROL | SISTER CAROL | HEART BEAT |
| 11 | 11 | GET ON UP | BAJJA JEDD | BREAK-A-DAWN |
| 12 | 28 | THE CURE | DON JAGWARR*** | PRIORITY |
| 13 | 12 | SCALP DEM | SUPER CAT | COLUMBIA |
| 14 | 1 | PUNNY PUNNY | CARLA MARSHALL | CHAOS |
| 15 | 15 | THE OUTLAW | PRINCE DORINIQUE | RADICAL |
| 16 | 13 | HERE COMES THE HOTSTEPPER | INI KAMOZE | COLUMBIA |
| 17 | | FROGS | CARLA MARSHALL | EPIC |
| 18 | 18 | MY WAY OR THE HI WAY | TONY REBEL | CHAOS |
| 19 | 30 | LET'S GET IT ON | SHABBA RANKS | EPIC |

| 100 | LC | TITLE | ARTIST | LABEL |
|---|---|---|---|---|
| 21 | 37 | SLY | MASSIVE ATTACK | VIRGIN |
| 22 | 22 | BUBBLE MI | RANKIN SCROO & GINGER | CRUCIAL YOUTH |
| 23 | 23 | TREAT THE WOMEN RIGHT | TERRY GANZIE | PROFILE |
| 24 | 21 | SIX STREET | WGIIL-A-GIRL | CHAOS |
| 25 | | SI WE...CHARGED FOR | SNOW/JUNIOR REID/ | EAST WEST |
| 26 | 25 | MR. MONEYMAN | SISTER CAROL | HEART BEAT |
| 27 | 27 | I AM WHAT I AM | MAD LION | WEEDED |
| 28 | 28 | WHO IS JAH | SISTER CAROL | HEART BEAT |
| 29 | 29 | LOVE WOMAN SO | MAD LION | VP |
| 30 | | WHO IS JAH? | RANKIN SCROO & GINGER | CRUCIAL YOUTH |
| 31 | | SILENT NIGHT | KOFI | BIG BEAT |
| 32 | 31 | AFRIKAN THING | KOFI | INTERNATIONAL |
| 33 | 34 | NICE & NAUGHTY | CHEVELLE FRANKLIN | RCA |
| 34 | 34 | VINEYARD PARTY | SUPER CAT | SONY |
| 35 | 33 | SLAVE TO THE MUSIC | RAYVON | COLUMBIA |
| 36 | 16 | WE DEAL WID ANYTHING | JR CAT | SONY |
| 37 | 35 | MISS TYSON | SUPER CAT & NICODEMUS | COLUMBIA |
| 38 | 36 | WE PROGRAM | JUNIOR CAT | COLUMBIA |
| 39 | | WE THREE KINGS | KOFI | BIG BEAT |

Get it up
I mean give it up fool
now give me those minerals
and those jewels
because it's me
the E on the attack
and I'm back with this jackin
comin up on some products that I'm lackin

Well I'm that other
ruthless type of brother
oh you aint heard about my antics?
shit
I ran cliques
through history
that left the US frantic
get us all romantic
before they fuck us

# TAKIN' THESE

"Takin' These" is another fantasy sort of song about what, how, and why, in the final hours of a mass movement turned revolution, how that might look and why it might happen. So you know, it's trying to get across the idea that we're talking about material things when we talk about revolution. We're talking about, not some sort of pride, not some sort of different way of thinking—maybe that's included—but we're actually talking about material resources that are created by the people but not justly distributed. — BOOTS

A Coup show in Jack London Square, Oakland. Thrown by Khalid Wilson, 1994.

got a hand trick
with a glock
for them bustas

Four hundred years ago
fool
where is my dough?
the year is '94
black folks aint taking it no more
We on the rise
The Coup is now the bad guys
you know
taking from the rich
giving it back to the po'
so put your two-faced ass on the floor
and get real
i can't feed my family with a happy meal

to the rescue but not long ranger with
    the lasso
i got the 9mm pointed at your asshole
so mr. IBM
give it up smooth
cuz this time all of your bowels gonna move
see it's a family thing

so don't even trip
my cousin JD got the nine
and my mama got the extra clip
so please oh please oh please give me
    them Nikes and free cheese
and while you on them knees break me
    off of my G's
cuz

Chorus
we are taking these if you please
cheerio
we are taking these if you dont please
check it out

knock knock muthafucka let me in
i just wanna kick it in your big-ass den

and if you don't like it take two to the chin
and show me to the kitchen cuz my kids are
    getting think
I don't have to talk shit about packing a gat
    in fact
you could get fucked by any other
    muthafucka
where i live at
give that money here it's crystal clear punk
fuck that fiscal year junk
meet the pistol-grip pump
pistol-grip pump meet mr. Rockefeller
we finna take him out do em like Old Yeller
it's been too damn long this profits aint
    been mutual
that's why today it won't be business as usual

call me the repo man
im a make it equal and
im get you if I caint my little sequel can
i know your down with the klan
but you must understand
you did the crime
so now it's time to put this 9 in my hand.
so put the money in the bag and 86 the tricks
don't forget to add grits with those afro picks
and free licks on that ass
cuz my ass aint living fat
boots you got my back? where the fuck you at?

i'm getting ammunition out the
    Pinto hatchback
refer to this as operation snatchback
cuz I got the fat sack of hollow
    tips to distribute equally
so who's the niggas, thugs, and pimps
    you mention frequently
gank me with frequency now i know you
    got mail
and if my glock fails
take a sip off this molotov cocktail
oh—is that your Rolls Royce?
come off up them keys cuz we are

taking these
even if you don't please

how does it feel when you got no food?
took over the supermarket so the people
    wouldn't feel the mood
how does it feel when you got no cash?
how the fuck you think it feels when
    your pockets singing "make it last"?

i choose to rock the boat instead to rock
    the boat
we threw the mayor's body in the bay
to see if it will sink or float.
you try to be the mack to me
you can't—we got agility
we taking factories, production plants,
    and all facilities
we got a gang of muthafuckas who done ate
they wheaties
no peace treaties
you swimming in your own feces
screwed us
now you're through with us
and don't need us
shoulda used a rubber cuz this shit developed
like a fetus

16 carloads packed full of chicken
I'm riding shotgun and my trigger finger's
    itching
this shit is real we got the enfamil
finsta drop it off at the spot on 23rd and
    Foothill
I give a fuck if you the army navy or marines
Aint shit to lose cuz we broke but packing
    uzi magazines
I seen the po-po, pulled the trigger, and
    flipped him the bird
he's 6 feet in the dirt
cuz I guess he hadn't heard that

# GUNSMOKE

SATURDAY·OCTOBER 29
SCHOOL
THE COUP and SPECIAL GUESTS
plus DJs
Mind Motion
Pause · Rolo 1-3
Ivan and Rize

628 DIVISADERO (THE OLD KENNEL CLUB)
SF · 21 W/ID · 415-931-1914 · ADVANCE TIX
AT BEHIND THE POST OFFICE, ZEBRA
RECORDS, AND GUE'S RECORDS

"I don't remember this show. It says it's at the Old Kennel Club in SF, which is now the Independent. Must be about 1993." — BOOTS

This is a song off *Genocide and Juice*. I did the music first—a real bluesy sort of take. You can find that riff in five million blues songs. It was "hard" as we like to say. At the time, Spice 1 used to work at UPS with me and E-Roc. We were all doing demos, and Spice 1 was in a group with Del Tha Funkee Homosapien called TDK, but Spice 1 became a multi-platinum-selling "gangsta rapper."

And we both first had songs on this compilation called *Dope Like a Pound or a Key*. I mean, that was in '91 or so and it was put out by Pizo the Beat Fixer, who was Too Short's DJ. Spice 1 got on this other independent label, Triad or something, and started to put out a whole bunch of stuff, and he blew up. A lot of his songs literally had the phrase "murder murder murder, kill kill kill," and they were tales of people killing each other. The beats were usually raw and we loved them all over the Bay Area, California, and the South, maybe even the Midwest like in Detroit and Chicago. People were bumping Spice 1.

He's the first person to make "gin and juice" popular in a song. It was something that kind of came out of the Bay

## GUNSMOKE

I be havin homicide runnin through my mind
Don't know what's up with me
shit fucks with me
all the time
eatin at my spine
A muthafucka in my prime
how you gon get yours
when you're too busy getting mine?

Now who is this
murderous
criminal
comin through?
if you think it's E-Roc
then the subliminals
is workin on you
it's thirty million of us buried in the fucking sludge
handcuffs never budge
I got a bloody grudge

Dead bodies lyin all around me
but the real murderers
aint never got no bounty
county
coroners
be spittin out statistics
lick this
ass if you think the blast
is coming from my residential district

There's something that I think you should know
is The muthafuckin Coup
we from the eastside O
peep my flow
creep by slow
see all my folks is broke
survival's for the cautious or the loc'd
take a whiff and smell the gunsmoke

I'm getting white hairs
from the nightmares
everynight

"This was me meeting Ice Cube for the first time at KMEL Summer Jam 1993. We snuck in with fake laminated passes. I mention this in the song 'Sneakin In.'" — BOOTS

GENOCIDE AND JUICE (1994)

Area, people talked about gin and juice all the time. That was popular in the Bay Area and in California way before Snoop made his song "Gin and Juice." When we named our album *Genocide and Juice*, it was in reference to this popular drink, not Snoop's song.

Anyway, back to Spice 1. The connection to Spice 1, he knows it, because his voice is actually scratched in by Pam in the bridge of the song where it says "back to the morgue." You can also find me in Spice 1's video for "Dumpin' Em in Ditches." And of course Spice 1 is also on this same album. Spice 1 and E-40 are also on "Santa Rita Weekend."

In "Gunsmoke" I wanted to write a song that was in some ways similar to what I thought was the appeal of gangsta rap songs. These songs were edgy and hard because they were talking about death and destruction. In some way it felt empowering because they were dealing with their problems, a lot of times in a very forceful way. Because of a lack of movement going on in communities that I grew up with, this spoke to the feeling of fighting back; the feeling of having taken power over your life. Unfortunately it was with the wrong enemies in mind, and with the wrong idea about what caused the problems. Many raps that are considered "gangsta rap," a lot of those rappers, including Spice 1, used to tell me that they were kicking "knowledge," that they were kicking game, that they were spittin' science, and in their mind they were trying to help the listener get through life. Anyway, I wanted to write a song with this edge—that talked about some of the same things, but from a different perspective. "Gunsmoke" is that song. — BOOTS

BOOTS RILEY

"THESE SONGS WERE EDGY AND HARD BECAUSE THEY WERE TALKING ABOUT DEATH AND DESTRUCTION."

## GUNSMOKE
{CONTINUED}

cause somebody's got a contract
on my life
I'm in a gang that's in an all out war
they jumped me in
when they knifed my umbilical cord
so it begins
with a slap on the ass
now you in the workin class, trick
you here so fast?
we already made your casket
wallet gots one buck
so the phrase "guns suck"
gets hella tired
gats ain't the only muthafuckas gettin fired

Skeletons deep down in the ocean
cause them slave ships had that three stop
motion
face-down floatin on the mississippi river
burnin crosses and
muthafuckas sayin "Die, nigga! Die, nigga!"
it all started when we stopped producing
scratch
some of my homies
got no legs attached
without no food up in the fridge
you aint go never have peace
cause with a trigger
you can finger fuck without no grease

I said
"Fuck the whole judge and the jury!"
my mind got delirous

my eyes got blurry
had my uncle strapped to the chair
hands ox-tied
breathing in gas
breathing out carbon monoxide
whole system stank like a load of bile
cos aint no billionaires
on a murder trial
made the ghetto concentration camps
every mile
so march your ass to the gas chamber
single file
who's the biggest problem that they show
on the TV?
more peoples die of starvation and T.B.
see me
with a angry face and a beanie
cause my relationship with Uncle Sam is
steamy
it's what I been through
I'm like Cinque
what I got
you got to get it
put it in you
the ruling class was cut-throat
since fresh off the boat
show em we aint no joke
let em choke
off the gunsmoke

# THE NAME GAME

172

BOOTS RILEY

"The Name Game" is a song I wrote in response to the reaction we got around town, around Oakland and other little cities in the US after we had videos air on BET and MTV. Oakland is kind of a small place and I'm sure that the ratio of artists to population is pretty high compared to other places. But there are a lot of artists in Oakland. And we were seen at the time as big fish in a small pond—everyone looked at us and saw: one, we were a symbol of success and two, our lyrics represented them, and there was a genuine appreciation for that.

Some of the effect of this was that people looked at us as an example of what is possible for people within capitalism—it made us into one of the false models that showed if people just strive hard enough, they could have a successful life. In reality, me and E-Roc, the other rapper in The Coup at the time, were really struggling to pay the rent. I lived in a small apartment at the time that was probably 300 square feet, and E-Roc had kids and lived in a place that wasn't much bigger. And we both had problems making ends meet.

There are a number of reasons for this. Even though we were number two on BET *Rap City* or whatever, we couldn't get shows, we couldn't get good-paying shows, because wherever a promoter might want to bring us, the police in that city would shut it down before we got there saying that it was going to be "too rowdy," there were going to be fights, things like that.

And these were shows that happened on our own at the time, you know, booking agents weren't getting us shows or anything like that. And the records didn't pay what they needed to pay. We didn't have other jobs, but still we were barely making ends meet and struggling. And I

## THE NAME GAME

Now
muthafuckas done made a name for theyself
But a name don't mean wealth
let me up you on the shit
If we was up in this just to get up out the ghetto
Let me tell you right now
We'd damn near done quit
I spit game on a regular basis
now everybody lookin at my hand like I'm holdin all the aces
Cool that they know our faces
from different places
But you cain't ketchup if you don't know what the Pace is
Everywhere we go
you know especially in the O
we hear "Coup! Coup!"
you know we got love fa sho
But even more
when they see us on B-E-and-T
and M-T-and-V
but me and E can't pay the P-G-and-E
Power come from the barrel of a bucker
I use the mic so that we aim at the same muthafucka
Cause your shit could go gold
and the only cash you got
is the silver kind that don't fold
I'm gettin bold when they ask
about the road that I passed
my peoples really be thinkin they gon come up fast
and they can rap and shake they ass
You ain't the first muthafucka who done schemed and scammed
and planned to scram
up out the ghetto
let me break this down from keys to grams
fuck the videos with the Benzes
and the cellular phones
spendin hundreds like quarters
The Benz is they partner's
the money's on loan
and um
"The cellular number you have reached is out of order"

Now
muthafuckas done made a name for theyself
But a name don't mean wealth
let me up you on the shit
If we was up in this just to get up out the ghetto
Let me tell you right now
We'd damn near done quit
Now
muthafuckas done made a name for theyself
But a name don't mean wealth
let me up you on the shit
If we was up in this just to get up out the ghetto
Let me tell you right now
We'd damn near done quit
I mocked Rockbox
wearin socks
in my basement
told my pops
I finna have as much mail as they got
not
I still plot to keep my cash clot flowin
My mind is bent on the rent
I'm barely makin it microphonin
It's true
it's a few gettin fund expansions
It ain't like Acorn Projects gon move into mansions
Straight authenticized shit
over synthesized hits
With this misty-eyed wit
to make your teeth grit
And I'm not tryin to diss like it's a bandwagon trend
They sellin six-packs
of them ways out the ghetto again
In the 20's it was boxin
the 50's doo-woppin
It's 1994 and everybody's star-hoppin
And ain't nobody really tryin to hear me speak
They too busy watchin Luke
gettin interviewed by Robin Leach
So if your mind is hooked on higher economics
Just kick it with The Coup
smoke this dub sack of phonics

wanted to explain some of the music industry to folks.

There were other folks in the music industry at the time who were lying about their income, which still happens to this day, to a certain extent. But you'd see pictures of rappers on TV in their houses, and in reality the houses were ones that maybe someone with a good union job could get. In the rappers' cases their income was a lot less steady, and although they might be shown in this house, be shown with this car that they were making payments on, by that time next year they might not be able to afford that same house or car.

However, we were becoming part of this Horatio Alger story that kept people from fighting the system and so I wanted to address some of that stuff in "The Name Game." And I also wanted to address some of the guilt that I was feeling when people would come up to me and say that I inspired them because of my politics to put a lot of energy into rapping. I started realizing that the example I'm giving to folks is not to organize, because I'm not organizing, I'm sitting here rapping. And so of course if people admire me, they're probably going to want to rap.

Now I realize that that's not the case; many organizers involved in everything from campaigns to actual battles with the police have told me how much my music inspired them to do what they're doing and how the music got them through those periods. But this guilt and this thought about what my art does, the effect that my art has, that guilt and that doubt led me to, after this album, quit rapping for a while. — BOOTS

"We won some award for being 'Most Socially Conscious' which didn't excite us." — BOOTS

The Coup:
   Comprised of rappers E-Ro
Pam the Funkstress, The Coup
"most socially consciouss" cat
and socially consciouss in this
the most profitable thing to be
a joke", laughs E-Roc with Boo
about a year and a half record
Juice", spending all our mone
going to bed hungry".   Even
The Coup then had to face rej
over their video, "Takin These
"They said that they were unc
message....but they're not unc
of naked women or people s
billy jam

## THE NAME GAME
{CONTINUED}

Now
muthafuckas done made a name for theyself
But a name don't mean wealth
let me up you on the shit
If we was up in this just to get up out the ghetto
Let me tell you right now
We'd damn near done quit
Now
muthafuckas done made a name for theyself
But a name don't mean wealth
let me up you on the shit
If we was up in this just to get up out the ghetto
Let me tell you right now
We'd damn near done quit

I'm gon die before I lie
to my peoples on the block
It's like frontin you gon shoot when you ain't got no glock
You bet not
that's a punk trick
this is how we run shit
I'm fittin to pitch a fit
cause I'm tired of hearin gums hit
Why do motherfuckers get up out and go for single
when the real high rollers draft a army to protect they Pringles?

Confusion
Here's a system based on prostitution
They done ganked you
don't be no stank fool with they solution
Unless you got about a million semi-automatics
you gon think you strivin doin them ho-style acrobatics

No I don't have it like that
Planned and plotted ain't got it
Keep my whole life savings stuffed in my back pocket
flock it

I'm scrapin fronts off like plaque
no slack
I come Realistic like Radio Shack
Intact
in fact
muthafuckas finally get they shit right
Ain't no fight
they scared shitless
all they do is grab the mic
Ain't no organizin real shit on the street
it's a fleet
of revolutionaries
in the studio makin beats
So fuck the fame
fuck the game
fuck the riches fool
I ain't got shit
unless all my folks gon have it too

Now
muthafuckas done made a name for theyself
But a name don't mean wealth
let me up you on the shit
If we was up in this just to get up out the ghetto
Let me tell you right now
We'd damn near done quit
Now
muthafuckas done made a name for theyself
But a name don't mean wealth
let me up you on the shit
If we was up in this just to get up out the ghetto
Let me tell you right now
We'd damn near done quit

oots and DJ
vedly won in the
Being politically
rap is not always
're still broke as
ing, "We spent
enocide &
e studio, and
ll of that sacrifice
from The Box
lains Boots,
able with the
able with images
g people"!

# SANTA RITA WEEKEND

**Santa Rita is a county jail in Alameda County.** It's based, I don't know, is the town called Santa Rita? It's near Castro Valley if it isn't in Castro Valley. I've been in the wrong place at the wrong time with some people who got into some trouble. I don't know what they were doing; anyway, they spent the weekend at Santa Rita and came up with the idea for this song. Originally it was going over the sample of Joe Sample's song called "In All My Wildest Dreams."

Tupac was actually supposed to be on it as well; we sent him the song, maybe he didn't want to do it, I have no idea, he did thousands of songs. Meanwhile, I changed the beat. We didn't end up connecting, but he ended up using "In All My Wildest Dreams" for "Dear Mama," which is one of my favorite songs of all times. So if he didn't appear on this song and that was what came out of it, that's great.

## SANTA RITA WEEKEND

It's like
Yale
mail
weights and scales
it don't mean shit when you sittin in the county jail
is it my turn
to tell the tale
of how I got popped
and how my lawyer failed to get me out on the spot?
slide the cell block
my homies give me love
some here for having gats
some here for selling dubs
sometimes you do your shit
and aint no second tries
look around
it's hella muthafuckas that I recognize
oh, whats up, man?
I'm back again
but its a temporary situation
takin weekend vacation
government incarceration
I call myself working on a pay hike
they calling me working on my third strike
psyche
I can't go forward
and motherfuckas can't ignore it
cos all my peoples
on parole
in the pen
or got a warrant
so its some shit i done leaped in
damn
another Santa Rita weekend

**FREE Thick**

November 1994      Volume 1 Issue 4

**THE COUP**

ALSO...
MIC GERONIMO
DREAMS OF PRODUCING A R&B B!TCH

Anyway, I came up with this beat, and it was kind of a weird little thing, that started with me building from a sample that sounds like but is not R2D2 squealing on the *Star Wars* soundtrack. Anyway, we built it off that. We came up with this crazy thing; on the actual version it has E40, Spice 1, and E-Roc.

And the song in my mind is about how the prison system, whether it's the penal system or the prison-industrial complex, has a hold on folks even when they're not in jail. When you might just get caught up on small charges every so often and you're living your life in fear of going back to jail. You know, because people have to do little hustles to survive because there aren't enough jobs. This came from conversations in jail and conversations in life with people. It's because people know that part of them making a living will have to do with them going in and out of jail at some point, as if jail is part of the community.

So that's basically what this is about. The song is called "Santa Rita Weekend." There we go. — BOOTS

scratchy guitar samples wh Drew Black and Cisco (and Kool Kim!) come with the rugged (but not too rugge flows ta get ya in that whylin' mood.

Overall, a worthy produc not classic material, but worth the loot if you can find it.

—tru

# Albums

## AWOL

### Detroit 4 Life
### Bryant Entertainment Group

AWOL (Afro-centric Wick Old-school Lyricists) is a thr man crew from Detroit consisting of B-Mack, Soul Man, and DJ Homicide. On *Detroit 4 Life*, the group combines both East and We Coast styles to form an album that should satisfy th fans from both coasts or th heartland.

The best cut on the albun "Gets 'em On," is an all-out assault on the pseudo-gangsta trend of the last couple of years: "We got gangsta-gangsta, madman

Oakland, 1993.

d at the same time
oviding a respectable voice
r the Detroit scene.
-josh ortega

**he Coup**
**enocide And Juice**
**ild Pitch**

**Genocide and Juice,** the
llow up to The Coup's
pressive 1993 debut **Kill**
**y Landlord,** is definitely
e of the year's three best
bums (along with Nas...
ru). The Coup (Boots,
oc, and DJ Pam the
unkstress) packs the album
ith intelligence and insight,
hile at the same time
lowing the music of the
e strings and horns to ease

major corporation an
businesses. While there, he
overhears some interesting
conversation between a
C.E.O. and the mayor of his
city. "We put up the funds
for your election campaign/
And, oh um, waiter can you
bring the champagne?/ A

real estate firm says
opportunity's arousing to
make some... most of
low income...
Immediately, we need some
media to say...
...gonna... these residents/
then we bring in the police/
Harassing every... ... ...ur/
they look inebri ted. ...
we buy the land,
motherfuckers will
appreciate it/ Don't worry

J.P. Getty and Norman
...
speak of how they "pimp"
the poor people. The song is
both gritty and frightening.
"Takin' These" tells of how
...
the rich giving it back to the
poor as they repossess
...of... capitalist
And for all West Coast fans
the hood...
California and the Sant...
Rita Weekend," in which
they...lif tal s o...the...
trip to the penitentiary.

...Said...H...e
establishes the...
most important
...gi...product...
...est Coast B oo E-
Roc, and Pam are walking in
...
...tov n pre e n x.
Black Panthers, in bringing
knowledge to the i...
knowledge which the i...
city can use to fight against
th...e real... rm...
The Coup...
important to be slept on.

"THE SONG IN MY MIND IS ABOUT HOW THE PRISON SYSTEM, WHETHER IT'S THE PENAL SYSTEM OR THE PRISON-INDUSTRIAL COMPLEX, HAS A HOLD ON FOLKS EVEN WHEN THEY'RE NOT IN JAIL."

# REPO MAN

Who is that muthafucka rollin through the hood?
Who is the muthafucka up to no good?
Who is the muthafucka takin your bank?
Who is the muthafucka always on the gank?

Now who's that muthafucka rollin down my street?
Every other week
jackin shit while you sleep
Creepin through the cuts
heartless
don't give a fuck
if you broke
Did you pay last month's car note?
Oh
I be scrapin
scratchin for bones
I got the cellular phone I just picked up on loan
Keepin up with them Joneses
put my ass in debt
Now who's the muthafucka tryin to take my shit?
It's the Repo Man
addin interest rates
He's got "BRKYOSF"
on his license plate
He took my color TV
the dining room set
The microwave
my daddy's Corvette
If you in debt
he's gon get yo ass for somethin
I heard
it's no future in yo frontin
So let it be known
Black folks don't own
they just give us this shit on loan

Who is that muthafucka rollin through the hood?
Who is the muthafucka up to no good?

Who is the muthafucka takin your bank?
Who is the muthafucka always on the gank?

Seen him slidin through the town
about eleven o'clock
A 1994 50
and the tires were stock
He'll make a visit to your house
like without no knock
And if you pulls out a pole it wouldn't be no shock
I gives a fuck how much you bench press
if you ain't pushin up
that twenty-five percent interest
your property gets chin checked
Reposessed
now your ride is at the shoe department
Dress For Less
He gives a fuck
if you's a mobber
with three toddlers
and a infant
He'll take the TV and the carpet in the living room that's stain
resistant
It's like living in the house
wit yo daddy
perchin nice
You can own a chair
but it's still Pop's merchandise
and ain't no gettin up and movin outside
The Repo Man got clientele worldwide
But trip on this
when you think you step ahead
Cause most likely
you one paycheck ahead
of the Repo Man

Who is that muthafucka rollin through the hood?
Who is the muthafucka up to no good?
Who is the muthafucka takin your bank?
Who is the muthafucka always on the gank?

## INTERROGATION

I aint seen shit
I aint heard nathan
I don't know what happened
I dont speak Pig-Latin
I'm a muthafuckin true
and it's us
against you
so
   fuck Starsky, Hutch,
   and Inspector Clouseau
   I was taught:
   don't rely on pigs for protection
shit
   I try not to even ask 'em for directions
   you're in the wrong section of the hood
   for a crime to be inspected
   got this block infected
   you could get ejected
   expect it
   ain't no love when you're The Fuzz—
   I mean—
   the fizz—
   I mean—
   my daddy told me who you was—
   I mean—
   The Wiz—
   I mean—
   You Can't Win
   Ease on Down the Road
   we got a Don't-Talk-to-Cops code
   I won't fold
   workin' for the man with the electric chair
   that's why I never watched Baretta
   and I hated Huggy Bear
   even Scooby-Doo snitched
   with that hippy-ass van

but me
I know the scoop
I know the plan
ask me no questions
I'll tell you no lies
you know the deal
the real criminals be dressed in suit and
ties
who holds the wealth?
You do more damage than help
so
   for me and my folks
   we gonna just do for self

*Rollin down tha street, ain't smokin indo, speakin on genocide and juice!*
but now everyone dies. Oakland has many hip-hop groups but this is one

**Thick:** What is different about this album compared to your debut?
**DJ Pam:** This album is tighter, allot of the stuff was edited until it sounded right.
**Boots:** Well everything has advanced the production, the lyrics, the concepts. We came and worked on it for a year and a half. We went back in and changed the things we didn't like and all the things like that you know. We basically just got better. The concepts, we came with some crazy concepts but still we kept it down to earth. Stuff like that. You know its just a step up on every level. It's kinda like we got more complicated and simpler at the same time. Like for instants with our beats we got more live instruments; we got string sections, horn sections...
**DJ Pam:** We had stand up bass and a drummer too.
**T:** Are these people from the local jazz scene?
**DJ Pam:** Yeah, we had some known musicians come in.
**Boots:** Yeah, and we used more tracks, we

# KILL MY LANDLORD (1993)

1. DIG IT!
2. NOT YET FREE
3. FUCK A PERM
4. THE COUP
5. I KNOW YOU
6. I AIN'T THE NIGGA
7. LAST BLUNT
8. FUNK
9. THE LIBERATION OF LONZO WILLIAMS
10. FOUL PLAY

***NOTE:*** This album contains work that I didn't like by the time the album came out. **It was my first serious attempt at lyric writing. Much of the album comes off more like a political pamphlet. The song "Foul Play" is one I wrote when I was eighteen or nineteen and is pretty bad as far as I'm concerned. However, this album receives a lot of retrospective critical praise. I guess these writers were in high school when this came out.** — BOOTS

# DIG IT!

presto
read *The Communist Manifesto*
guerrillas in the midst
a Guevara named Ernesto
so
what a brother with a Afro know?
yo, dough'll flow for the mack
and we the ho
so grow
cause they're lynchin
brothers might get hung
Rhetoric
flowin from the tip
of my Mao Tse-Tung
deficit
money spent
catch the glint
of my nine
as they cut welfare 25 percent
and I dissent as I clench and raise my fist
we did away with that
so you could get with this
here's a twist
cause we'll overthrow like Kwame Nkrumah
Spread around the wealth
as if it were a vicious rumor
Pam cuts the record
like a surgeon cuts a tumor from a brain
we're all cooped up
so feel the pain
from 400 years of exploitation
anesthesia provided
by your local TV station
patience
is not a virtue
I ain't waitin'
turn this shit over like Bush did a boatload
    of Haitians

how now brown cow
I'm down with the Mau Mau

clown
downtown tried to put us in the dog pound
like H. Rap Brown
grip the situation
won't get no callouses
cause we're spittin dialectical analysis
so how is this
we never had no funk
until you found out that our trunks had
revolutionary hump?
chump
bump you over like dominoes
rat
So free Geronimo Gi Jaga Pratt
lyrics
hear it
fear it
can't get near it
got a sample
didn't clear it
Point Blank says "Fuck 5-0"
That's the spirit
Cheer it
spat out the fat that I consumed
Knew that I was doomed
since my date of birth
to be the wretched of the earth
never had a dream that was American
there goes the electric chair again
despair again
But that ain't nuthin new
Told the streets were paved with gold
Whoever paved that shit
got minimum wage too

gunned us
stunned us
exploited and they hung us
I'd like to take a moment to say "Fuck
    Columbus"
millions off my back
the Black-on-Black crisis is a myth
The crack

that did the damage
was the one from the whip
the record skip—
the record skip—
the record skip—
the record skips cause my voice is kinda
    scratchy
from yelling "Don't shoot!"
when 5-0 comes to harass me
they never pass me
no one to go and tell bro
tryin to kill the movement with the new
    Cointelpro
Leaders they killed
if I said it
it would credit em
They only see my back because I'm
    three steps ahead of em
we're not fallin in the slot you slated
we realize
that our power is nickel-plated
masses move
as well as asses do
class is through
our time is over past its due
and you still wanna know
the origin of the flow?
Oakland, California 94610

## NOT YET FREE

In this land
I can't stand or sit
and not get shit thrown up in my face
A brotha never gets his props
I'm doin bellyflops
at the Department Of Waste
And everyday I pose a front
so nobody pulls my card
I got a mirror in my pocket and I practice
   lookin hard
I'm lookin behind me
beside me
ahead of me
There'll be no feet makin tracks here instead
   of me
But I can't disregard
just what the news says to me
I'm 21
so I've reached my life expectancy
At any minute I could be in some shit
that kills my skinny ass
from muthafuckas doin the sellout strut
or probably Oakland Task
My relationship with OPD
has been like one big diss
Long arm of the law grips my dick so tight
it's hard to even piss
Oh I forgot
ain't even got a pot to do it in
Up at the church
they're tellin me it's because I live in sin
So I grin
but nevertheless my mind won't dwell
I must be trippin
cause I thought I was livin in hell

Capitalism is like a spider
the web is getting tighter
I'm strugglin like a fighter
just to bust loose
It's like a noose

asphyxiation sets in
Just when I think I'm free
it seems to me the spider steps in
This web is made of money
made of greed
made of me
Or what I have become
in a parasite economy

In the winter
there's a splinter
with the smell of the rain
And the scent of the street
but all I smell is the pain
Of a brotha who's a hustler and he's stuck
   to the grind
Of a sista who's a hooker
gotta sell her behind
Desperation makes a brotha get a little more
bold
The circumstance gets deeper
when it's damp and it's cold
So I spend my time thinkin bout the
   ultimate gank
Can I get my crew together
pull a move on a bank?
I'd be the picture perfect hustler for the
   piece of the pie
But my daddy always taught me
just to reach for the sky
Now my dreams and aspirations
go from single to whole
As I realize there's a million muthafuckas
   in the cold
No need to be told
cause when you got a million po' people
Gettin ganked
by a few that are rich and evil
But it's illegal
to wonder how they livin fat...
1, 2, 3
everybody get a gat

Niggas
Thugs
dope dealers and pimps
Basketball players
rap stars and simps
That's what little black boys are made of
Sluts
Hoes
and press the naps around your neck
Broads
pop that coochie
Bitches
stay in check
That's what little black girls are made of
But
if we're made of that
who made us?
and what can we do to change us?
The oppressor tries to tame us
here's a foot for his anus
Well
since the days when I was shittin in diapers
It was evident
the president didn't like us
Assassination attempts
I'd root for the snipers
My teacher told me that I didn't know what
   right was
Well
she was wrong
cause I knew what a right was
And a left
and an uppercut too
I had a hunch
a sucker punch
is what my people got
That's why I was constantly
red, black, and blue

# FUCK A PERM

The short version of this song is on the album, but then we did an extended version remix I think on the flipside of the "Dig It!" single. I wrote it while I was going to San Francisco State, so even though I considered myself a communist, I think that there was definitely a lot of the nationalist aesthetic in politics rubbing off on me. Mainly because I was making it my mission to get some of these folks, who I thought could be good organizers, to have some class analysis in what they were doing. And I mean cultural nationalism. A lot of what was talked about was hair and identity and all that kind of stuff. I think that combined with the fact that at the time I had a fade with dreads on top, basically short on the sides and long on the top, twisted in dreads. I would get a lot of shit for it. So I made a song that in my mind was a response to that. Later on when the song got recorded I had an Afro. And so it was also in response to the negative feedback I was getting around town for having an Afro. In the song I'm going on about hair textures and its meaning and people's view of themselves, which I think is important to address, but

## FUCK A PERM

Apply three drips
rub softly with your fingertips
And even though you flipped
don't trip
cause now you're hip
And now you slick it
you grease it and you lick it
and you're lookin' really wicked
but your hair is now called good
You're moisturizin'
texturizin'
relaxizin'
civilizin'
but yo
I got a 'fro
so a bro's misunderstood
kitchen in the back
give me dap I got a nap-sack
knick knack Patty's wack
cause in her mind it's firm
that straight is in
and out is black
cause black went out with tenament shacks
but beauty is a natural fact
so I say, "Fuck a perm!"

Paris, 2003.

one of the reasons I included this on this album had to do with the crowd that was there at the time and some of the cultural nationalist trends that were happening.

So, that being said, when we did our first tour to promote this album, we were going every place, and at every show—it was funny it would work like clockwork because we didn't even have to plan it. We'd come out and do one song and somewhere before the second or third song, somebody in the crowd would say something funny about my hair like, "Man, you know, get a perm." You know they'd say that or, "Cut that shit," or whatever. And that would allow us to respond, hit right on cue, come with this song "Fuck a Perm." When we did this tour it was 1993, and in the Bay Area and in a lot of places, for the most part, people had stopped wearing curls or perms and things like that. Some people still did it, but it wasn't the norm. However, when we got to Milwaukee it was, and this was back in the days when our crowds were 95 percent Black. And so although it was 1993 in Oakland, the styles looked like it was 1984 in Milwaukee. The Starter jackets, which had stopped being in style at that time (now they're back to a certain extent), and the curls. Everybody, most of the crowd, had curls or perms, this is my recollection. So while we're on stage E-Roc had said to me, "Whatever happens do not do 'Fuck a Perm.'" So I thought that was sage advice. But, we did a good show and then we get off stage and are signing autographs in the parking lot, and somebody from far away is like, "Hey, Coup!" (pronounced "coop" because a lot of people call us Coup with a *p* and I didn't really care because as long as they could see the name of the group and get the album, it worked). "Hey, Coup!" and then we looked up and there was a group of

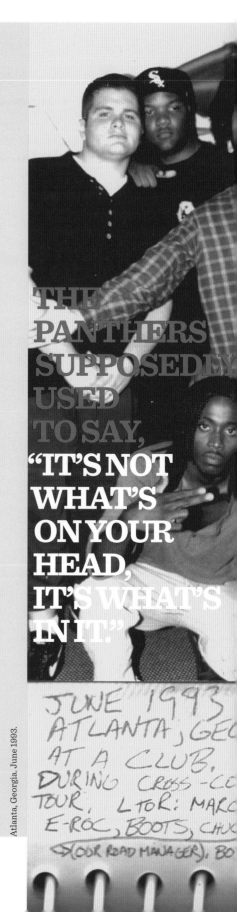

THE PANTHERS SUPPOSEDLY USED TO SAY, "IT'S NOT WHAT'S ON YOUR HEAD, IT'S WHAT'S IN IT."

Atlanta, Georgia. June 1993.

JUNE 1993 ATLANTA, GE AT A CLUB DURING CROSS-C TOUR, L TO R: MAR E-ROC, BOOTS, CHX (OUR ROAD MANAGER), BO

like six dudes with curls and they were like, "'Fuck a Perm'? Fuck *you*." So obviously, we hadn't done that at the show; they must have heard the album, heard the song, and felt offended. By the time we finished signing autographs, we're all going clubbing. They're in their car *blasting* the album, bobbing their heads and they're really into it, but every time we come up close to them, they're like, "Fuck a Perm, Fuck *You!*" But they're bobbing their heads, follow us to the next club, and to about three different clubs, and it occurred to me that they love the album and love what the music was talking about. They're blasting the album, they're bumpin' it, and I realize the song kind of had, that it's connected to a certain kind of politics, that says in order for you to be revolutionary you are going to have to change yourself. In order for you to join the movement you're going to have to start from the inside. And there are versions of that in cultural nationalism, there are versions of that in hippie new-age stuff, and that's not actually what I am putting forward. I'm putting forward the idea that a material change in the way wealth is distributed will then change the culture. And that we also know that culture does derive from material situations. If you are in a fishing village where you have to survive by fishing, there are going to be cultural things that have to do with that. Everything comes out of that, and I realize that also, that is not the idea that I want to put out, that's putting people's energies in the wrong places. I'd been around some other wrong approaches and I think that song, that experience, changed a lot. I think that experiences like that kept our music relevant because the rest of my music wasn't preachy from then on. The other songs weren't about you changing yourself, they were saying,

"Hey, we can all see what's wrong. Let's go get them, let's go change the system." And I think that's what kept our stuff from being ignored. Still, I always felt bad about that because they were bumping the album for two reasons: 1) They just really liked it and they were happy to be around us or 2) They wanted to show that this was an album that could have been for them, and there's something really offensive about the lyrics. I want everybody to join a revolutionary movement, and hopefully that empowerment will help you make your own decisions. I heard a quote that the Panthers supposedly used to say, "It's not what's on your head, it's what's in it." And that was probably their reaction to some of the cultural nationalist trends that were happening at the time. — BOOTS

BOOTS RILEY

"At a show at San Pablo Park Recreation Center in Berkeley. The event was put on by the *Black Panthers Commemorator* newspaper. Left to right: me, E-Roc, A *Commemorator* volunteer, and our old DJ, DJO." — BOOTS

"I HAD TO KEEP THE 'FRO AND SIDEBURNS SO PEOPLE WOULD PICK UP THE RECORD AND BE LIKE, 'OH, THAT'S DOPE.' I LOVE THE STATEMENT THAT I'M MAKIN' WITH IT. BUT IT'S NOT WHAT'S ON YOUR HEAD. MY APPEARANCE SYMBOLIZES SOMETHING, BUT MY APPEARANCE IS SECONDARY."

—BOOTS, INTERVIEW BY FRANK WILLIAMS, APRIL 2000

# THE COUP

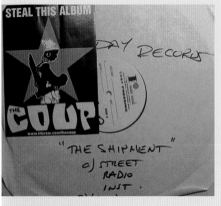

## THE COUP

*Dick Doolittle:* Yes, I would like to speak to Boots from the rap group The Coop.

*Boots:* It's The Coup, and this is Boots. Speak.

*Dick Doolittle:* Well my name is Dick Doolittle and I'm a reporter from Grime magazine and we would like your comment on the tragic riots—

*Boots:* Not a riot, it's a rebellion.

*Dick Doolittle:* Well, the tragic rebellion?

*Boots:* Man, tragic for who?

*Dick Doolittle:* Well there's havoc in the streets, the police have lost control over the people, criminals are running free from jail, and people are actually taking property from big businesses, it's complete chaos—

*Boots:* That's not chaos, that's progress.

*Dick Doolittle:* Mm-hmm. OK, is that your comment?

*Boots:* No. This is it.

[hangs up phone]

Check it out
It's the muthafuckin C-O-U
To the P
now you're fucking with the real dudes
Who will meet you with a fleet of brothers in the street
Getting drunk off liberation
fuck the Hennessey
Cause you clowned and kept us down
for far too long
Now you're going up in smoke
like Cheech and Chong

And the song "I Ain't the Nigga"
is the Constitution
Niggas die but Africans make revolution
So what happens
when a people do not get their dues
Well let's try it
There's a riot so flip on the news
And let's go east to 98th
here in Oaktown
But let's just say
for story's sake
that it's in your town
A hundred brothers taking factories
one was Laura Scudders
And now they're handing out free chicken
and free peanut butter
Free food to the people
how it should be
But now let's go a few blocks over to 7-3
Channel 2 says at the mall
twelve cops got shot
Cause there's eight hundred sisters taking
    over Eastmont
With nines and AKs
doin the right thing like Spike Lee
And now their babies got free Pampers
and free Nikes
Up at the schoolhouse they said
muthafuck a hall pass
Until you teach the truth
check it
we ain't going to class
You're teaching lies
we got wise
now we realize
There's no end to this road
you disguised the prize
So peep game
for real mental penetration
Our education's liberation

At 6-9
There's a rally and it's swinging
Through the crowd
with a thousand voices singing
Once upon a time in the projects, yo
Muthafuckas took over
and now we running the show
We don't give a damn about section eight
    though
For what we really need
We're gonna have to take mo
The same thing was heard in the Acorns
In Campbell Village
across the bay in Fillmore
And in the hills
where all the rich folks live
They're in shock we're not Bell, DeVoe, and
    Biv
Instead of brothers on stage singing "Do me"
A black man
has a gauge singing
"Do this, see?"
All of a sudden everybody is out of jail
But it's funny
cause nobody is out on bail
And somebody shoved some police against
    the wall
I guess today
they shoulda worn their clean draws
Cause an ambulance came
That's the reality
There's now a new meaning to police
    brutality

All we need is satisfaction
We don't want just a fraction
And we've come to
A conclusion
Revolution is the solution

Check it
Now the Uzis
that were once used to kill each other
Are now used
to serve and protect the brothers
And the sisters
cause they're packing .45s and nines
We're down for revolution
not just down for their behinds
Cause the word is heard across the bay
    and in L.A.
In New York, NY
Chicago
and Atlanta, G-A
We gives a fuck if you got money and
    the millions
Cause muthafucka we got posse in the
    billions
So break yourself Bush
It's collection day
Break yourself Trump
It's collection day
Break yourself DuPont
It's collection day
You stole the shit from my great granddaddy
    anyway
The liquor stores around
but they're not sellin beer or ale
Muthafuckas sellin Molotov cocktails
To the crew
so light up a brew
And this is what is meant by a goddamn coup

# I KNOW YOU

Los Angeles, 1987. May Day March.

## "I'M GIVEN RATION
## ON THE FIRST
## AND FIFTEENTH
## JUST SO I WON'T B
## OUT ORGANIZIN IN
## THE STREET

# I KNOW YOU

I know you muthafucka
know where you live
You're the cop that knocked in my partner
   Greg Wiggins's ribs
And it wasn't in the Trib
cause he's not a dealer or a pimp
But now he walks with a permanent limp
And pig
you make my gut crimp
cause a whole family got knocked
Rossy Hawkins and her sons
up in Double-Rock
And it don't stop
to the funky beat
Till my people get together
and kick you pigs off the street
I grit my teeth
why can't I be like Rodney with a camcorder?
Seems we need one
every time you get a court order
Or pull me over in order
to check identification
I'm in the back of your car with a bruise or
   laceration
You're in the hood
and it's one more disaster
We know you're here to protect and serve
   the master
Next time you roll through
press the gas a little faster
I'll turn your blue suit purple
bastard
Cause I know you

I know you muthafucka
Your footprints in my door
On my back
on my head
through my house and once more
You called my mother a ho

threw my brother in a headlock
You did this to about six houses on the block
Say you tryin to stop the rock
so it makes me perspire
Hmm
but you work for the supplier
So I inquire
what's your role in my elimination?
Ain't got a choir
so it sure ain't one of salvation
But if I sung you a song
it'd be of damnation
Cause all they let me do is sing in this
   damn nation
Hey hey hey
hey hey hey
how many kids have you killed today?
Pig
now I realize our relation
Your occupation
is to keep me in occupation
How many brothers have you left in a cast?
How many graves have you made in the past?
Useless
Not my task to even ask
But you'd better cease
before I put a cap in your ass
Cause I know you

I know you muthafucka
my face prints in your knuckles
Hit my head back to the rear
and I can hear my knees buckle
And you chuckled
as the blow
blurred my vision
You make a game trying
to tame me for colonialism
The stars and bars are all you need to make
   a perfect prison
No chains or fences here so you can make
   me think I've risen

I'm given rations
on the first and fifteenth
Just so I won't be out organizin in the street
And so I'm beat and in the court
with charges trumped, see
My eyes is swollen
and my nose looks like Humpty's
But I'm not laughin
cause I'll take a bath in this one
The judge is looking at me like he wants to
   have me hung
I never swung
I got the dung kicked out my ass
Like O.P.D.
was using me for Beat-the-Nigger class

Step one: put the handcuffs on
Step two: say something like "Nigger you're
   gonna learn"
Step three: throw em down on the ground
Step four: kick em, of course

But there's an error in your reign of terror
and your end is near
We ain't non-violent no more
so get your riot gear
Stand in fear
and guard your rear
as we gather round
And fuck you up so much
they'll have to fuck you down
Assuming the position
that you'll have to wear a bullet-proof vest
On your chest
I suggest you change your address
Cause we know you

Main photo: "1990, Oakland. For a little while, I was a party promoter.
This was for a party called 'Underground Cafe.'" — BOOTS

Inset: Cover of the single for the song, "Funk."

# I AIN'T THE NIGGA

# I AIN'T THE NIGGA

step into the world of a nigga

figure

to stay a little while

so pack your bag up bigger

first of all

just let me introduce you

seduce you

into a frame of mind that's easy to get used to

Nigga hasn't always meant a man with melanin

it used to be a piece of wood

that sat on the cotton gin

masta put it there

and it wouldn't move

smooth

so what does it mean to be a Nigga With an Attitude?

you tell me that a nigga's crazy or lazy

not about the skin

so

don't let it faze me

well you amaze me

with that ignorant bizull-shizzit

get a grip on the new fit

cause that's a lame frame of brain for the nineties

I know the game so it don't stain my mind

see

so what the fuck

you wanna race for the trigger

I ain't the one

I ain't the nigga

nigga

is a word we use today

you say

It don't mean the same if you spell it with an A

but that's an argument that makes me itch

I twitch

if I took the T out would I still mean bitch?

my name is E-Roc

and I ain't the nigga mayn

save your sellout-strut shit for Soul Train

cause I've been known

to knock a motherfucker out

without a doubt

The Coup gives me much clout

but there's a factor when I know that my skin is brown

and never ever will I put another brother down

so I make the mental rule to massacre the word

cause when I hear it

it gets me straight stirred

it's mental trash

so I'm pickin up the litter

I ain't the one

and I ain't the nigga

my people use this word each and every day

you see a nigga? slap a nigga

that's what I say

my attitude is this

don't call yourself a nigga bro

unless you're just an oakie-doke

it'll make you sicker though

cause it's all about a mind-tame mind-frame

the system is a chess game

we're pawns all the same

until we change our mind to rough from raucous

identify yourself

it's a part of being conscious

if I call myself a gangster then I'll rob you with a gat

if I call myself a brother then you know I got your back

if I call myself oppressed then I'm clear on where I'm at

but if I call myself a nigga what the fuck is that?

don't be the coolie or the moolie or a boo with the jigga

don't be the one

don't be the nigga

# LAST BLUNT

Last night
I puffed on my last blunt
damn that was a stupid stunt
cause I done said this ten times before
that when my life has come to a crescendo
I would let that Indo go
but I'm still kissin it
like I'm under the mistletoe

So here we go
I'm walkin with the steady swagger
speakin with a st-steady stagger
preachin with a Southern drawl that sounds
like Jimmy Swaggart
coughed and played it off
Said I know I'm slippin
See
It's the last one G
my laces are tied
so you can't trip with me

I remember
1988 December
Someone said "Puff on this before you go up
in her"
So I did it and I guess it must have did the
trick
She enjoyed it so I guess I must have rocked
the clit
Felt like a man and I left there with an ego
trip
Don't know why
cause I couldn't even feel my dick

Ego trip lasted and I'm always gettin blasted
but it's drastic
cause sometimes that shit can help you get
your ass kicked
Can't buy it with plastic
so I'm off to drain the bank for dank
I get complaints
cause the neighbors say my house stank

Call myself a saint
cause I won't touch the brew or Boones
I gives a fuck
just don't interrupt my Looney Tunes
this afternoon
cause I could find a job anytime
Step off my behind
I'm in a Doobie Brothers state of mind
Run-D.M.C.
AT&T
yo they both be illin
I smoked that blunt
for last month's
three hundred dollar billin
And I'm willing to admit
that when provoked
I smoke to cope
but if I didn't take a toke
I'd be leadin a street revolt

So I make a mental note
and to my frustration
I decide I can't do shit about the situation
Put the spliff to my lips
flick the Bic
and it's on hit
Coulda been my last blunt
but I cain't quit
cause then I have to deal with
some motherfuckin real shit
Squeezin me tighter than you gotta squeeze
a cow's tit
But on the flip tip
I know I gotta get a grip
even though in high school
it used to be hip
But shit
I'm hockin spit
like I thought it was worth somethin
My throat can't take no more
no future in my frontin

But it's rough
when you grow up

and the tough men roll joints
That's why I been on a binge for marijuana to
this point
But it don't faze me though
I take it lackadaisical
It takes a while for ways to grow
and get out of the old flow
But I'm an old bro
I done passed two decades
I'm wearin shades
so my eyes don't reveal the red haze
caused by my younger days
like Frankie Beverly and Maze
I'm Back in Stride Again
no roaches
and no safety pins
Now I'm pennin rhymes about gettin on the
wagon

and I get skittish
when I think of how the British
put the opium in Asia
backflip to that tactic
Gankin black folks while they daze ya
if you're gettin perved
you're gettin served
it's economics
like the gin and tonic
Brothers get moronic
from that chronic bionic
and it's ironic
cause we're not gettin fucked up-
we're just gettin fucked

Shit out of luck
and we're stuck
with our mind in a muck
So don't duck
the situation
cause I used to smoke fat Taylors
til I figured out that the ganjah was a jailor
Wait a
minute
while I get up in a funky situation

The Coup is coming through and there's no

hallucination

So what the fuck

they say that junk

is good for meditation

If you smoke a sack

take some Ex-Lax

it's mental constipation

there's no hesitation

when I'm talkin bout


political friction

Stoppin evictions

Government made afflictions

and I have an addiction

that's a big contradiction

so I must confront it

Cause

ain't no revolution gonna come from the

blunted


My partner's cousin's uncle

got killed by a shooter

I'm depressed

so there's a rumor

Boots is gonna hit the buddah

Mary Jane

will be alone tonight

the only type of hit in sight

comes from Pam the Funkstress

give it to her

Images from *Thick*, vol. 1, issue 4, November 1994.

BOOTS RILEY     DJ PAM THE FUNKSTRESS

WWW.ILLCREW.COM/THECOUP

# PAM THE FUNKSTRESS

e new Coup back for round two. Last time they was scheming on the landlord
has game and a goal. So check the message, the live instruments and the ill

Anytime there's some new growth area in culture or anything in capitalism there's going to be a lot of people trying to figure out how to make money off it. Sometimes that's record labels and other times that's promoters and sometimes it's folks say, "Let me show you how to make money off of this." So there were so many, so many conferences, it just seemed like one a month. Conferences with three people sitting up there telling you what order to put the songs on your demo tape, telling you what A&Rs are looking for, what makes a hit song. They're still doing that right now. There's a conference happening somewhere this weekend that's charging people $50 to tell them that. So we used to go to these conferences. Sometimes you could even get lucky enough to pay to get a spot to perform. So I think that we did a few of these conferences and another group that was doing it at the time was a group called Funk Lab All-Stars. They had a deejay named Pam the Funkstress. We would see her perform a lot and at a certain point I heard that they weren't all working together anymore and I saw Pam deejaying at Tupac's first album release party.

I just came up to her, and I think we already had a deal ready to go; Wild Pitch had already approached us. And so we knew Pam from these events, and we knew how good she was and started working with her. She may not have known, but we knew we had a deal already in place, so yeah, we just kind of stole her from everybody. I'll tell some stories and see. She should be okay with this.

I remember we were on the road early, right after the album came out. We had this road manager whose name I won't mention because whatever. But a lot of times bands get on each other's nerves. We were four people, me, E-Roc, and Pam, and a road manager in a minivan for like a bunch of weeks. People do play the dozens, they cap on each other. I had seen enough of this in the rest of my life to know to stay out of this. But something happened between her and the road manager where things were said and it went from playing in the van to really

being an all-out something. When we got out of the van at our show in Houston, Pam had an uncle that was there and I guess he didn't know exactly what had been said, but Pam and the road manager were yelling at each other. They were yelling at each other and her uncle was there, and we went and got on.

Because back then it wasn't a band and we could just kind of get up on stage. Everybody would just say, "Hey, tell the soundman to turn the mikes up." That was the sound check during the show. And a good fifteen minutes of your twenty-minute show was set aside for doing that. And so we got out and we were doing the show and I looked over to the side and there's a dude that has a gun held to the head of our road manager, and it's Pam's uncle. Apparently he's saying to him, "If you ever—" I don't know, he didn't know exactly what was going on or whatever, he was like, "If I ever think that you might hurt my niece, you are going to have me to deal with." And he's just sitting there and Pam stops the music and says, "Yeah, that's right, motherfucker" into the mike and then starts the

"I WANT TO LET THE FEMALES LOOK AT ME AS A ROLE MODEL. I WANNA LET WOMEN KNOW THAT THIS MAY BE A MALE-DOMINATED FIELD, BUT WOMEN CAN DO THIS!!!"

~PAM THE FUNKSTRESS, *RAP PAGES*

music back up. So that was one of our earliest touring memories with Pam. I'll ask her if that's okay for me to put this in here.

The other thing about Pam is that she was one of the technically best deejays in the world at the time. She was winning all sorts of contests, but her reasons for getting involved in deejaying is because her friends were deejays. She had a lot of male friends and they were deejays and she wanted to hang out with them. As she started getting better and winning these contests, she's having contests against people that she wants to be friends with, and they were getting mad, and not being friends with her and giving her dirty looks. So she'd win a contest and be crying because people are like, "Oh fuck that shit," and they were who she wanted to be friends with. There are videos of her at these battles and she just didn't want to do that anymore because, and I don't think that there was that sort of animosity outwardly toward the dudes that won, but you know, I would imagine it has to do with someone thinking they couldn't get beat by a "girl," by

a woman, and they had to show out or claim that it wasn't fair or this or that. So, you know she stopped doing those competitions because she got emotionally hurt by her friends when she won. Some of these things are maybe for her to tell.

I talked about in the explanation for "Me and Jesus the Pimp," how I wanted to make a song that spoke to sexism but from a standpoint that I could see it from. Not that there's reverse sexism, but how women being oppressed actually makes life terrible for everyone. That's the idea behind "Me and Jesus the Pimp in a '79 Grenada Last Night." But I think other ways that it comes out in my music are just not necessarily as thought out. The song to my daughter ["Wear Clean Draws"] was me actually just wanting to make a song for her. At the time when I started writing it, she was an only child and we were about to have another child, so I wanted to write something to her then that was how I was thinking of her then, knowing that it would be something she would listen to later on. I didn't see it necessarily as an

antisexist or a song with feminist ideas; it's just ideas about the world that I'm relating to her. So I don't know. There's another song on that same album, "Nowalaters," which is about something that happened to me and I wrote when I realized that I had come to a different understanding of the events. Yeah, I think those ideas that I have are informed by the world and wanting to make a world in which people are empowered and that has to do with addressing issues of sexism. It also has to do with appreciating people for their human potential. That all goes together.

I think early on, definitely with the first album, there was a lot of talk of "We need a song that talks about this, we need a song that talks about that," because you know you're young and trying to think of things. I kind of go with other concepts and other situations, and I talk about them, but I talk about it from every angle and I think about them holistically and those ideas are just going to come out of me if I'm being honest and real. — **BOOTS**

# FUNK

I used to kick it with a brotha named Moe
Moe used to kick it with a brother named Joe
Joe used to kick it
with his girlfriend Lakeisha
whose brother Elmo
looked like me
Elmo used to elbow lots of brothers in the
nose
Kick em when they down
and then he'd steal their shoes and clothes
Elmo would develop lots of beef as a tweeker
and all of Elmo's foes would come lookin for
me
Imagine that
fat muthafuckas with bats
tryin to rat-pack?
Hmm
time to get a gat
So I'm strapped cause I'm trapped
like Roger Thomas
in his fat mama's lap
What's Happenin?
here's the rap
Saturday
twelve o'clock
told E-Roc the whole plot
and what not
about
how I'm in a spot
he said
"There's ten of em
you'll get spread like frostin
you ain't Steve Austin
Elmo got tossed and
Boots
maybe you should move to Boston"
But you get lost when
you're played like a punk
Pile on the Right Guard
I got serious funk

Bet George and Bootsy never had funk like

this
Catch-22 twist
no fist can dismiss
this riff that I'mma go through
maybe I can flow through
this whole ordeal
and not pull out the black steel
and my friends make suggestions
that I should squeal to the cops
but that's out of the question
If I die by the trigger of a misled brother
could he be judged by the system that has
killed a billion others?
I believe no
so I don't go with the flow
even though I'm bout to row with no paddle
up a creek called shit
light is lit on the situation
It's me or him gonna decrease the population
Now we wonder why a revolution never grow
Killin muthafuckas just for steppin on our toe
If we had as much funk for our oppressors
as we did
for ourselves
the blood would never flow again
And then
the Uzis that were once used to kill each
other
Could be used
to serve and protect the brothers
And the sisters and the cousins
or whatever others
But the funk keeps growing like a fungus

four years til I'm twenty-five
now I got a forty-five
caliber
don't take no jive
just for the fix
Don't want to be eighty-sixed
Route 66 ain't in my mix
Don't flap your lips about me takin no trips
You won't be takin no sips
from a milk carton

seein my face with a caption
askin
"Have you seen Boots? He's missing in
action"
This shit is more Off the Wall
than Michael Jackson
cause
brothers
do be doin brothers
who be doin others
screwin brothers
but The Coup be doin
more than shoo-bee-dooin
on the corner
talkin revolution from Victoria to Florida
that's why it don't make sense
that they want me a goner
on a run
cause some brothers in a rampage
think I'm poppin junk
and they don't see
four centuries
of genocidal funk
so I'm a punk
if I don't blast they ass
But I gots more funk for the rulin class
Will it ever end?
will we ever win?
drinkin juice and gin
5-0 kills again
gets off with a grin
National Guard sent in
but when we got beef you wanna pop the
trunk?
we got serious funk

# THE LIBERATION OF LONZO WILLIAMS

1986
a muthafucka doin tricks on the mix
and I don't mean the fader
Face of zits
but gettin grits with black steel firesticks
Tryin buildin empire somethin like
    Darth Vader
Now Lonzo was armed with nothin but a
    mean mug
But tugged a forty-five, with forty-five slugs
He was a jitterbug thug
at the dance cuttin a rug
Treatin the sistas like a hooker
Greetin his partners with a hug
Breakdown
Shakedown
this brother would take a pounds
of soon to be caked grounds
and then go make rounds
Firerods protected wads of gorgeous green
Paper stacks of paid tax off of broken dreams
At puberty his liberty was found within a key
Rocks were cookin
but he's lookin for a way to be free
Here's a key
there's a key
but Lonzo, where's yours?
There's no key to the door, but there's money
    on the floor
So stoop down
Bend over
Hurry, pick it up fast
But watch out, Lonzo
You'll get fucked in the ass

Knock knock
who is it?
time to visit
but it's two years late
Cause Lonzo's rollin harder and it's 1988
He's got some fat ends

got some more friends
and a brand new Benz
He's got respect and he suspects that it
    won't end
A couch is still a couch and a chair is still a
chair
But a house is now a crackhouse, Luther-
Lonzo's there
Dyin brains
dyin bodies
to and from this dead residence
Try in vain to kill they pain, exchangin
    dead presidents
petite bourgeoise, parlez-francoise?
I don't speak it but I know it
It's all the same
the business game, but you go to jail for
    this shit
We were tribal our survival was not based
    on stompin rivals
Who's the fittest as I raise my fist?
Some can't survive and not be ruthless
So while we scrape and scratch for bones
And a cellular phone
somebody's sittin on the throne
Cause they don't let Black folks own
They just give us this shit on loan

Madge says that Bounty
is the quicker-picker-upper
Well, Lonzo says the County
is the slipper, tripper, stuck-er
Years of unsettled funk
and who-gets-what-bunk junk
makes you feel like you took a test
    and flunked
But don't get disturbed or perturbed
the teacher's on my last nerve
plus he grades with a downhill curve
Told Lonzo kick it
the system is wicked
trick it
but dig it
We got a way to lick it

gave him a book
said "Here's the ticket"
Now he's addicted to learnin how we been
    afflicted
And what distributin that shit did
I made a quick bid
to say "Don't trip kid
You never worked for the mob,
you had a government job."
Lonzo knew I was right
no fight
now we're tight
Plus
he been out of jail about a year ago last night
Now he hangs with us for revolutionary
    ruckus
And 5-0
more than ever wants to fuck us
Just cause we know the road to riches is
    crooked and narrow
We'll get more power from a hundred
    thousand gun barrel

From the video for "Funk,"
directed by Abraham Lim.

# FOUL PLAY

Left: Cover of The Coup's EP.

# FOUL PLAY

Brothers on the block making bankroll
The billion dollar dream
is the dream of the cash flow
Little do they know
they're a little or a big ho
But they have a car
they can side at the sideshow
I'm the type of brother
that'll tell another "Hell no"
To the sellout-strut
hockin rocks in a hellhole
brother you can slide
you can glide
in your hoo-ride
But you're gonna drown
in the high tide of genocide
Brothers give my five but it's live jive
Can't understand
that their hands in a beehive
I'mma take a risk on the disk
take a big dive
Just to make it rhyme on time I'll say
"Overdrive"
Missed 'em
I'm not with them
but they're victims
Cause they're just a part
not the start
of the system
No hocus pocus
that's the focus of the song
Hope that you can learn this
and one day sing along
A clearly cut case
co-opted by The Coup
An exposé of foul play against me and you

Explicit
and implicit
are the exploits
I'm speaking of society that's living off me
No jobs from coast to coast and into Detroit

Now I am a factor
that they don't need
Cause labels
are stable in this big world
Talking bout sex
you're a boy or a girl
Talking bout a con
you're a jerk or the jerker
Talking economics
you're the boss or the worker
Right about now I'm gonna change the flow
Going straight up
like my new wave afro
I say it and they play it
Do you hear me though
you're guessing there's a lesson
But teach me
I want to know
Conjunction junction what's my function?
Connected with the genocidal pace of a race
reduction
Funny there's no money
for my people's production
The Coup is not through
cause we've got some gumption
A victim in a system about cold cash
If you don't make it
then they treat you like trash
Dispose of you tonight if not in the morning
This is not a prophecy
this is just a warning
A clearly cut case
co-opted by The Coup
An exposé of foul play
against me and you

At times
I find my mind can think fast
Like when a pig has a trigger
saying nigga that's your ass
Thoughts of a slave master rise from the past
The past is the present
cause I still feel the lash
It's against the law just to be black

Cause the war on drugs
is just thugs on the attack
The C is not the source of course so just get
back
Why try a lot, I doubt it's just about crack
Brothers on the block making bankroll
Maybe could the dream be the dream of an
overthrow?
If so no mo' we'll play the big toe
In a shoe that's cramped so break a brother's
sole
Slip and stuck slowly to the same game
Several hundred years we have been in a
chain gang
Let our shackles only add on to a migraine
Old fame, thoughts of pain slowly drive me
insane
But then I started rapping for The Coup
A lot of rappers out there just looking for the
pay-off
Listen to the message that the Boots brings
to you
The Coup is just a group to bring order out of
chaos
People pick problems out and isolate
Misguiding many to think it's a mistake
Well I'm the Boots and I'm here to set 'em
straight
My information leads me to think there's foul
play
A clearly cut case co-opted by The Coup
An exposé of foul play against me and you
Sing it

It's funky, it's funky, it's funky, it's a funky
situation (x3)

# THE GHETTO BLASTER EP (2010)

1.    GHETTO BLASTER
2.    THE NEW FUCK YOU
3.    SCARS

# THE GHETTO BLASTER EP

*The Ghetto Blaster EP* was the second release by Street Sweeper Social Club. **Production-wise and musically, I think it started hinting at where we could have gone with that project.**

The first album was made up of a lot of riffs that were classic, unmistakable Morello riffs. It also was recorded at a fancy studio with Stanton Moore on drums and Tom on bass doing the basics and then overdubbing everything else track by track after.

We recorded *The Ghetto Blaster EP* in a one-room studio at Tom's house, with the whole band playing and being recorded at the same time (the band was now five of us—me, Tom, Carl Restivo, Dave Gibbs, and Eric Gardner). The band had also toured together and was extremely tight. There was energy there that wasn't on the first album. I also think that the new songs on the EP—some were covers—were more of a melding of styles between me and Tom. Or we just got more used to each other.

I've always had both serious and humorous sides to my work. Working on the first SSSC album was an interesting challenge for me because I saw Tom's riffs as heavy and serious. This made my writing tend to stay on the heavier side for most of the album. By the time we did *Ghetto Blaster*, the riffs had changed some to accommodate the humor that's often in my work. — BOOTS

## GHETTO BLASTER

Shotgun sonata
From personas non grata
With a plot to rock harder than the
    second intifada
I do drink firewater
But I'm more like Hiyawatha
And we'll slaughter, slaughter, slaughter
    your armada
Inform your scholars that our alma
    mater's squalor
So my squad'll pull your collar at your
    black-and-white gala
We're canon fodder for dollars
Both under Bush and Obama
I'm not a baller
I'm a brawler
Callin y'all to come harder

Cuz I'm a Ghettoblaster
See, I'm a Ghettoblaster
Yeah, I'm a Ghettoblaster
I'm a ghetto
I'm a ghetto
I'm a ghetto
I'm a Ghettoblaster

I'm from the land o' the free labor
That planted the plan of the
Black-and-branded to scram it
Over to Canada

A fan o' radical bandits and bandanas
Who slam in the banana clip
And rat-a-tat-tat-tada

They spat the grammar ta

Scam y'all to clamor up
The damn ladder ta
Grab for Excalibur
Not a rap battler
But the next caliber
Catch the program and
Not just my pentameter

Cuz I'm a Ghettoblaster
See, I'm a Ghettoblaster
Yeah, I'm a Ghettoblaster
I'm a ghetto
I'm a ghetto
I'm a ghetto
I'm a Ghettoblaster

C'mon and help me out
Need y'all to help me out
C'mon and help me out
Help me out
C'mon and help me out
Need y'all to help me out
C'mon and help me out
Help me out
Cuz I'm a Ghettoblaster
See, I'm a Ghettoblaster
Yeah, I'm a Ghettoblaster
I'm a ghetto
I'm a ghetto
I'm a ghetto
I'm a Ghettoblaster
Cuz I'm a Ghettoblaster
See, I'm a Ghettoblaster
Yeah, I'm a Ghettoblaster
I'm a ghetto
I'm a ghetto
I'm a Ghettoblaster, muthafucka

THE YOUNG COM
HOO-RIDE AT T
CITY COU

STOP THE NO CR

UE. JULY 9TH, 6 PM
NEAR 14TH & B'WAY)

AT CITY HALL

he Revolutionary Comrades
Collective is inviting all
our folks to the
continue the
struggle against
he no crusing
aw at Lake
Merrittt set off by
---- the Police day. We are
aking this fight
o the Oakland

Coked out is the new tipsy
Tracy Morgan's the new Nipsy
Skinny jeans are the new fashion
But none of that shit fits me
Weed smoke is the new incense
Two bucks is the new ten cents
3 strikes is the new lynchin
Buyin is the new rentin
These lines are new molotovs
Right now there's a new holocaust
More troops is the new call it off
I'm tryna pry this collar off
Hip Hop is the new rock now
Curfews are the new lockdown
Gunshots are the new cricket chirps
Let's flip this shit top down

Fuckin is the new "Hey, how do y'do?"
And revolution is the new fuck you

The New Fuck You
The New Fuck You

Flagwaving's the new seig heil
Do nothing's the new denial
Torture is the new torture
We'll all walk that green mile
The dope spot's the new factory
Nip/Tuck is the new quackery
Handguns are the new switchblades
And freedom's the new fantasy
"Get a room" is the new "get a home"
Low income's the new hella po'
Phone sex is now group sex
There's feds on your telephone
"Take care" is the new health care
Big business gets welfare
The Middle East is the new gold rush
We've made a new hell there

Fuckin is the new "Hey, how do y'do?"
And revolution is the new fuck you

The New Fuck You
The New Fuck You

209

THE GHETTO BLASTER EP (2010)

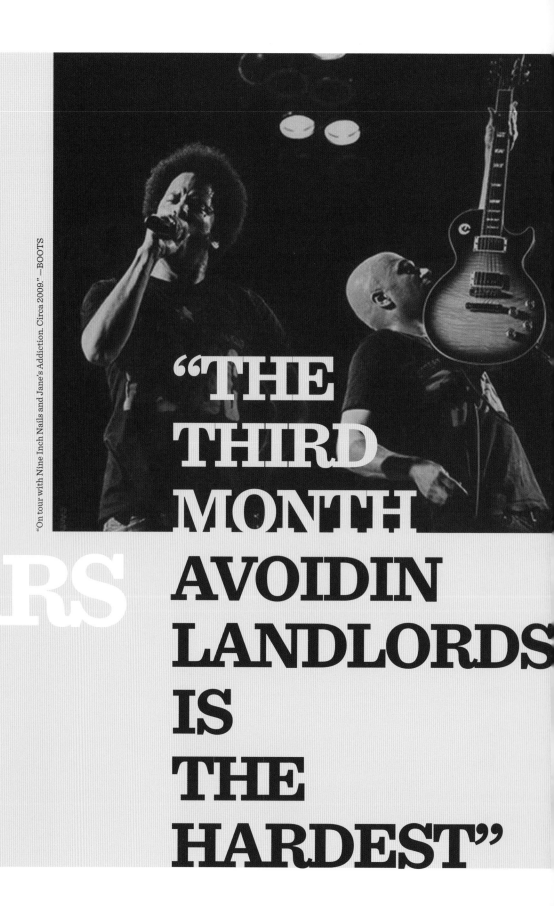

"On tour with Nine Inch Nails and Jane's Addiction. Circa 2009." —BOOTS

# SCARS

## "THE THIRD MONTH AVOIDIN LANDLORDS IS THE HARDEST"

## SCARS

Had a car with stuck doors and primer finish
To take a girl out I had to climb her in it
She really hoped her friends didn't find her in it
When she wanted two drinks, I said "Mind yer limit"
Show up at the party, new suit and Stacys
Very next day, return it back to Macy's
Say it smells like sweat? Sir, is you crazy?!
Gimme my refund or push up daisies
Me and two friends used to share a pager
So every three days I would swear I'm major
'lectricity from the next door neighbor
broke muthafuckas be sharp as lasers
I was more tore back than a stolen car tag
Just used somebody else's card for the bar tab
A dollar hot dog wasn't nothing to bark at
It's only funny cuz you don't see where the scar's at

Scars!
Hold that pose!

Got free cable cuz I know somebody
Got some broke patnahs that'll throw somebody
Not pickin up the phone cuz I owe somebody
Got a twamp note I'mma photocopy
A date with me was all kinda fun
Go to the restaurant, dine, and run
The bank might keep declinin' em
But these hundred dollar checks, I'm signin 'em
The rubber on my sneakers used to flap when walkin'
It looked like two little muppets talkin'
"Ay, w'sup baby? Do you come here often?
Oh, I got some new shoes. They just haven't been brought in."
This old ripped jacket is cuz I'm an artist
I'll burn rubber on you if my car will get started
The third month avoidin landlords is the hardest
It's only funny cuz you don't see where the scar is

Scars!
Hold that pose!

welfare checks
food stamps
collection notes
broken amps
paycheck late
shut off notice
pyramid schemes are
hocus pocus

Hold that pose
Hold that pose
Hold that pose
and don't ever come down
Hold that pose
Hold that pose
Hold that pose
and don't ever come down

211

# STREET SWEEPER SOCIAL CLUB (2009)

1. FIGHT! SMASH! WIN!
2. 100 LITTLE CURSES
3. THE OATH
4. THE SQUEEZE
5. CLAP FOR THE KILLERS
6. SOMEWHERE IN THE WORLD IT'S MIDNIGHT
7. SHOCK YOU AGAIN
8. ORIGAMI (GOOD MORNING, MRS. SMITH)
9. MEGABLAST
10. PROMENADE
11. NOBODY MOVES TILL WE SAY GO

# STREET SWEEPER SOCIAL CLUB

Street Sweeper Social Club was born the day after Audioslave broke up. The key members in the band are me and Tom Morello. Tom came to a Coup show in L.A. where we were opening for Les Claypool. We had been friends for a few years at this point and had done many live acoustic collaborations. He said that he wanted to help the world come to know my work, and us working together on an album with his famous funk/rock riffs would do that. "Street Sweeper" is a slang term for an extremely dangerous weapon—a semiautomatic gun that shoots shotgun shells, twelve in three seconds. The name is based on a lyric from "5 Million Ways To Kill a CEO," *If you's a janitor—get a street sweeper.* Our logo is a boombox with cannons coming out of the speakers. The name, and logo, says we are using our music as a weapon. Not *the* weapon, as Fela says. That's bullshit. But it's one of the weapons. Organizing being the biggest one. — BOOTS

## FIGHT! SMASH! WIN!

And the wealth don't trickle down
People pinchin every nickel now
Even if we don't fight
bodies hit the ground
I spit the sound
of a million fists finna pound
I'm in the crowd til this whole thing
  switch around
Our brains are on temporary disconnect
I shoot my mouth off
I can't find my pistol yet
You can call this music disrespect
Cuz it'll slap you in your face at your local
  discotech
Mr. Green with your missiles and rockets
My paycheck burns a hole in your pocket
You told the judge put my name on the
  docket
Meetin in the break room
here's what we plotted

Chorus
Let's fight
Let's smash
Let's win
We gon fight
We gon smash
Let us in
Let's fight
Let's smash
Let's win
Just like gettin up in the club with a
  fake ID
If it don't work, we gon do it again

Your honor may it please the court
Swear me in on a book full of Tupac quotes
After what I say
you night noose my throat

Reporters please scribble down a few
  hot notes
Allow me to be the first
to throw dirt on their graves
Excuse me
I never learned to behave
my great great granny was a Carolina slave
she whispers in my ear
sayin "Spark the blaze."
Somewhere on the eastside of steal and rob
A whole generation got a McJob
And the light bill still ain't resolved
See the hungry mob pulse and throb
If you got a blacklist I wanna be on it
If we gon attack this then we need to run it
If you see my hood man
You might call it ghetto
Politicians are puppets yall
Let's get Gepetto

Let's fight
Let's smash
Let's win
We gon fight
We gon smash
Let us in
Let's fight
Let's smash
Let's win
Just like gettin up in the club with a fake ID
If it don't work, we gon do it again

Well it's a matter of fact that I'm gonna die
one day
But muthafuckas
Right now I breathe
And I may not be able to predict my demise
But you can bet it won't be on my knees
I'm rappin at the speed of the falling dollar
They got greed to make you crawl and holla
Its old school like Easy-E's Impala

Ay! Ay!
You gon lead
or smoke trees and follow?

Let's fight
Let's smash
Let's win
We gon fight
We gon smash
Let us in
Let's fight
Let's smash
Let's win
Just like gettin up in the club with a
  fake ID
If it don't work, we gon do it again

# 100 LITTLE CURSES

May you tumble and fall down your grand marble stairway
May that caviar pâté you were eating block your airway
May your manservant deliver the Heimlich with honor
May this make you vomit on your Dolce Gabbana
May your wife's worried face show a horrific expression
May you realize she's not worried—that's just Botox injections
May all the commotion cause to crash your chandelier
And propel into your rear
Its sharp diamonds from DeBeers
May your Ferrari break down
May your chauffer get high
And smash up your stretch Rolls up on Rodeo Drive
Off the breaking backs of others is where you got all your bucks
Til we make the revolution
I just hope your life sucks

All my people in the place put your fist in the air
All my down muthafuckas get up outta your chairs
All my real down peoples we got love for you here
cept for that muthafuckas right there

get em

May your Champagne not bubble
May your pinot be sour
May that white stuff you snortin be 96 percent flour
May the famous rapper you bring to your daughter's sweet 16
Get some pride and walk out
As if born with a spleen
May the death squads you hire be bad with instructions
And by mistake be at your mansion with the street sweepers bustin
May this make your party guests forsake their white Russians
And dive behind the Jimmy Martin
Cryin and cussin
May your chef be off pissin in the bisque in the kitchen
May I assume your autobiography is filed under fiction
Cuz off the breakin backs of others is where you got all your cash
Til we make the revolution
I hope your life sucks ass

All my people in the place put your fist in the air
All my down muthafuckas get up outta your chairs
All my real down peoples we got love for you here
cept for that muthafuckas right there

get em

From the video for "100 Little Curses."

STREET SWEEPER SOCIAL CLUB (2009)

# THE OATH

Video stills from Street Sweeper Social Club performing "The Oath."

## THE OATH

The lamppost could swear
it had seen me before
And stared
as I stumbled through the motel door
The dirty mirror
also thought I looked familiar
But commented only that my suit was
brilliant
The TV
bolted to the wall and cracked
Remembered how I cried
and said I'd never come back
In the lacquer of the table
I had carved my oath
With a burnt butter knife
And this is what I wrote

I pledge
to get their foot off my neck
Instead
I shall demand my respect
I'll fight
even if I won't win
Alright
the beginning is the end
I pledge
to make the bosses cringe
Instead
we'll get some justified ends
I'll fight
til the system is gone
Recite
this ex-losers song

(Yeeee!)
Alright, Muthafuckas!
(Coo-Coooo!)
Fight, Muthafuckas!
(Yeeee!)
Alright Muthafuckas!

(Coo-Coooo!)
Fight, Muthafuckas!

I pledge
to live life as lesson
That said
even my words are weapons
I'll fight
show love in motion
Alright
mountains move from oceans
I pledge
there is no surrender
Instead
I'll expose their agenda
Fight
and make vampires bleed
Recite
this ex-losers creed

(Yeeee!)
Alright Muthafuckas!
(Coo-Coooo!)
Fight Muthafuckas!
(Yeeee!)
Alright Muthafuckas!
(Coo-Coooo!)
Fight Muthafuckas!

I pledge
that I'll taste each second
That said
I know each moment's a present
I'll fight
a battle fit for ballads
Alright
at two we hit the palace
I pledge
that we are individuals
That said
from you I'm indivisible
Fight

and match the blaze of comets
Recite
this ex-losers promise

The carpet
inquired
if I'd lay there again
And where was the girl
from when there last I had been
The commode
refused to speak
as I made my escape
It knew every subtle nuance of my
    war torn face
The concrete outside
felt disrespected
It was partly my fault it had been
    neglected
At the precipice of fate
is where I carved my oath
With the dagger from my back
And you know what I wrote

(Yeeee!)
Alright Muthafuckas!
(Coo-Coooo!)
Fight Muthafuckas!
(Yeeee!)
Alright Muthafuckas!
(Coo-Coooo!)
Fight Muthafuckas!
Na na na na, etc.

STREET SWEEPER SOCIAL CLUB (2009)

# THE SQUEEZE

This brick
Which is gripped by my fingers
Which shoot out from my hand
Which is fastened to my arm
That meets up with my shoulder
That sits well below my head
That surrounds my brain
Which is tied up with thoughts of resentment, fear, and loathing
Because of your using me in your road to wealth and power
Will crash though your picture window
and kill you

We gon put you in the squeeze
We gon put you in the squeeze

The city is a planet of glass and granite
And it's ran by some masters of mack mechanics
We got schools where the facts are banished
We got scams where your stacks'll vanish
And the hospitals is gon cost you racks
so panic

All the gangsters throw your triggers up
All the stoners throw your flickers up
All the drunks throw your liquor up
All the bank tellers stick em up
Teach them babies how to grip a buck

When this hits the streets it's
thunder with thesis
We'll show where the beast is
Make sure it deceases
They smolder with speeches
We shoulder the leeches
Call off them polices
This ain't where the thief is

Janitors
Work all night like Dracula
Burger flippers grab your spatulas
Managers
Get your Acuras
Big bosses guard your sack because
We'll put it in the squeeze

Squ-squ-squ-squ-squeeze
Squ-squ-squ-squ
We gon put you in the squeeze
Squ-squ-squ-squ-squeeze
We gon put you in the
We gon put you in the

World poverty has just gone platinum
Unemployment checks
need to come with a gat in em
Chains and leather whips
Slave masters still crackin em
This is where I'm scattin from
Listen to the battle drum
We all got our shackles on

Ladies shoot your deuce-deuces
Bankers tip your masseuses
Wardens tighten up your nooses
Muthafuckas make noise if you bought your clothes boosted

The earth is composed of space and atoms
And controlled by some pimps
without Stacy Adamses
but one day they're gon taste the cannon
when the people rise up
and make them muthafuckas face the dragon

Mercenaries show your paychecks
Homeless folks show your blankets
Rich folks throw your banquets

Tell officials what to say next
Cuz they won't be at ease
When we put em in the squeeze

Squ-squ-squ-squ
We gon put you in the squeeze
Squ-squ-squ-squ
We gon put you in the squeeze
Squ-squ-squ-squ
We gon put you in the squeeze

Cuz they vote with their guns
Cuz they vote with their guns
Cuz they vote with their guns
Cuz they vote with their guns
Cuz they vote with their guns
Cuz they vote with their guns
Cuz they vote with their guns
You know they vote with their guns

C

"About midnight on the night of the Occupy Oakland general strike / port shutdown. Guy behind me with the beanie on is MC Hammer." — BOOTS

# CLAP FOR THE KILLERS

"There's still a lawsuit going on about this. The campus police deemed me too dangerous to speak on campus without hiring a bunch of police! I spoke at the Peace Center instead, which is not owned by the university." — BOOTS

Banned from Ca[r

"BUT THEY THE ONES WHO WROTE THE LAWS"

THE KALAMAZOO
PEACE CENTER
PRESENTS

**BOOTS RILEY**
FROM THE COUP

Speaking on Equality, Progress, and Action

**7 PM** AT THE BLAH DE BLAH

# CLAP FOR THE KILLERS

Now can you clap for the killers?
Give it up for them gangsters
One time for the killers
Double up for them gangsters


Well I
wrote this for criminals
But all of y'all should listen at me
Now if you ever catch me snitchin
just haul off and slap me
They on the other team
Lets rumble
is my thoughts exactly
They work for gangsters
and they whacked Fred Hampton Jr.'s pappy
Ay playboy
pop em with a pistol and get executed
Ay mama
murder em with missiles and you get saluted
Go head and
gank em for a grand
it's DNA computed
But bankers bathe in the Bahamas
Off of billions looted


Now can you clap?
Now can you clap?


Now can you clap for them killers?
Give it up for them gangsters
One time for the killers
Double up for them gangsters


Well I
wrote this for criminals
But they the ones who wrote the laws
They aint on TV gettin arrested all up in their draws
They stick their hands up politicians
make em move their jaws
And they be starving folks for bread

until their breath pause
Ay take a memo Moneypenny
Say the deed is done
And you can bcc DC
and say our leaders won
But first we fax the photograph of the opponent's son
Adjust the image
cuz it's hard to see the gag and gun


Now can you clap?
Now can you clap?
Now can you clap?
Now can you clap?


Now can you clap for them killers?
Give it up for them gangsters
One time for the killers
Double up for them gangsters


Well I
wrote this for gangsters
While I sprinted through your backyard
Not for them Coppola criminals
They just act hard
Tony Montana had a stylist and a SAG card
When he reloaded slaves forgot they had back scars


Ay
M-M-Mister DeNiro what kind of gun is that?
Can you look more like a menace?
Take two
now run it back
Ay s-s-so what Scorsese
got all them money stacks
Long as his lens never looks at
the real maniacs


Can you clap for them killers?
Give it up for them gangsters
One time for the killers
Double up for them gangsters

# SOMEWHERE IN THE WORLD IT'S MIDNIGHT

Somewhere in the world it's 3 o'clock
Time to get out of school and think
Somewhere in the world it's 5pm
And quittin time means it's time to drink
Somewhere in the world it's 8 o'clock
Let's get fly, man, and go to the gig
But somewhere in the world it's midnight
And the guerrillas just shot two pigs

Somebody needs to bottle
This adrenaline
Throw death the middle fin
Stompin through your suburbs
Like coke, meth, and riddalin
Streetlights and little sins
We fight for little yen
Despite the bitter end
And ignite carcinogens
This here's a little shot of
Can't-Be-Stopped
A little Fuck-You-Pay-Me
A little Fuck-the-Cops
Cuz them parasites'll suck your wop
And bankrupt your flock
Chuck you overseas to buck the glock
And in the gallows of San Quentin
The officials were smitten
By the smooth, suave way
Which my initials were written
So they paid no attention
That the scribbled transmission
Read "I'mma get outta here,
Pray I don't get ammunition"

Somewhere in the world it's 3 o'clock
Time to get out of school and think
Somewhere in the world it's 5pm
And quittin time means it's time to drink

Somewhere in the world it's 8 o'clock
Let's get fly, man, and go to the gig
But somewhere in the world it's midnight
And the guerrillas just shot two pigs

Sometimes the night falls just so
You can't see the scars
Discourse between the stars
Is dialogue of stolen DVD players and VCRs
I know a corner—if you say "cocaine"
They swear that you takin the lord's name in vein
I came to spit flames
Until the shit change
Until we switch games
The streets drown in pain
Now
Y'all might just drink and fuck to this
Let's knuckle up and deconstruct the shit
I'mma show you what they dysfunction is
They need some nickel-plated acupuncturists
Vile and vulturous
Let's get tumultuous
And bring a multitude
To where their luncheon is

Somewhere in the world it's 3 o'clock
Time to get out of school and think
Somewhere in the world it's 5pm
And quittin time means it's time to drink
Somewhere in the world it's 8 o'clock
Let's get fly, man, and go to the gig
But somewhere in the world it's midnight
And the guerrillas just shot two pigs

# SHOCK YOU AGAIN

They summoned
And I answered
Their Godforsaken call
Just focus on the names
Not the screaming down the hall
Your tears beg the question
why you're bound in this chair
It's simply because—
Ay, wait muthafucka
I'll ask the questions here!

Shock! Shock!
Shock! Shock!
Shock! Shock!
We gon shock you again!
Shock you again!

Shock! Shock!
Shock! Shock!
Shock! Shock !
We gon shock you again!
Shock you again!
Shock you again!

You tremble
You're sweating
You writhe around in peril
But let me assure you
my instruments are sterile
Forget those
electrodes
I placed inside your mouth
Just say what I want
or I flip this switch
And in Cairo the lights go out

Shock! Shock!
Shock! Shock!
Shock! Shock!
We gon shock you again!
Shock you again!

Shock! Shock!
Shock! Shock!
Shock! Shock!
We gon shock you again!
Shock you again!
Shock you again!

My name is Luc Mammon
I used to work with fire
Since hell came to earth and pain has worth
I put myself out for hire
For centuries my superiors have
inflicted pain
with skill
Electric is my pimp slap
I'll liquefy your will

Shock! Shock!
Shock! Shock!
Shock! Shock!
We gon shock you again!
Shock you again!

Shock! Shock!
Shock! Shock!
Shock! Shock!
We gon shock you again!
Shock you again!
Shock you again!

# ORIGAMI (GOOD MORNING, MRS. SMITH)

*Chorus*
In the military outpost known as hell
We was way too drunk off Muscatel
Prone to fail and get thrown in jail
From the stories that the TV was known
    to tell
This night at the end of the world
Police sirens sing to boys and girls
Handful of pills to press your curl
Baby shine that light
Let your fight unfurl

My confession is also my blessing
Hollered Hail Marys suckin on a Smith &
    Wesson
May salutations interrupt your isolation
I'm just like you
another profit calculation
I learned a lot
from things left at my apartment
Forgotten papers that you dropped on my
    carpet
Musical chairs
you thought your luck was just startin
Who told the record to stop?
Took the collection note you left at my spot
and made you
origami

Woo hoo
Good morning, Mrs. Smith
Woo hoo
Good morning, Mrs. Smith

In the military outpost known as hell
We was way too drunk off Muscatel
Prone to fail and get thrown in jail
From the stories that the TV was known
    to tell

This night at the end of the world
Police sirens sing to boys and girls
Handful of pills to press your curl
Baby shine that light
Let your fight unfurl

Dancin in my kitchen
with Sly Stone's permission
Lit my ignition
cursing fascist apparitions
You said your life was something like the
    Inquisition
All you could do was lay there in prone
    position
I said there's love inside the people
connectin
and interactin
strugglin
finding direction
That's why you see insurrection
here's some affection
We the targets of war
Took the eviction note they tacked on
    your door
and made you
origami

Woo hoo
Good morning, Mrs. Smith
Woo hoo
Good morning, Mrs. Smith

In the military outpost known as hell
We was way too drunk off Muscatel
Prone to fail and get thrown in jail
From the stories that the TV was known
    to tell
This night at the end of the world
Police sirens sing to boys and girls
Handful of pills to press your curl
Baby shine that light
Let your fight unfurl

I heard that power is the rum of the
    brain and
for us it's fixin
not just numbin
the pain
and I'm not just comin complainin
I'm just explainin
how this life is a blessin
I took the farewell note you meant for
    your exit
and made you
origami

Woo hoo
Good morning, Mrs. Smith
Woo hoo
Good morning, Mrs. Smith

## MEGABLAST

I am your host for the evening
Don't take the bullet out—leave it in
Intoxicate me til I'm bleedin gin
And I still walk straighter than them thievin
men
5 million ways to ho—choose one
Consider this game to go—use some
Stockbrokers pace the floor and do some
State fellatio and ooh um
Ay man fuck them Federallies
Muthafuckas can't get enough bread at
Rally's
Bringin white girl through Mexicali
Homies came up and got dead in alleys
Cocaine, soda, and H2O
Tryin to make the dough
Here's the hate below
With a statement though:
If we hustle for the state to go
Security'll brace the door
They can't take the blow
Of the

Megablast
Mega-Megablast
It's a Megablast
Mega-Megablast

My heartbeat vacillates to a faster rate
Thinking bout bills and scratch to make
Muthafuckas work til our back is ached
But calculate what massa take
Revolution Rock on acetate
They seein how much our ass'll take
How much money can them bastards make?
We gon wrassle fate
Tell em pass the cake

Some get drunk off Jack and baked
Yack in the back
Come back and drank
Some just mentally masturbate
Won't graduate from class debate
Point forty-four is the calibrate
But they'll replicate if we assassinate
Fuck big biz and their magistrates
Explode on the seen and smash the state
Megablast
Mega-Megablast
It's a Megablast
Mega-Megablast

Slumlords of the world have united
And they announced a world tour
You are hereby cordially invited
To the Third World War
Slumlords of the world have united
And they announced a world tour
You are hereby cordially invited
To the Third World War

Let's hit em with a

Megablast
Mega-Megablast
It's a Megablast
Mega-Megablast
It's a Megablast
Mega-Megablast
It's a Megablast
Mega-Megablast

# PROMENADE

Another SSSC promo.

"IS WE FINNA FIGHT OVER CRUMBS TO BITE OR MAKE A WHOLE MUTHAFUCKIN WORLD IGNITE?"

# PROMENADE

Now I got a new kinda square dance rap
Gon talk smack
Flash my gat
I'm finna spit and hold my dick
And heat shit up like a thermostat
Grab your partner by the chaps
Give your partner a pimp-slap
To symbolize the ghetto trap
Step to the right
Give three claps
Kids jam-packed in tenement shacks
Aint shit cookin on the stove but crack
This is the bat this hell begat
Cuz bosses are cleptomaniacs

Two by two
Promenade
Duck from a B-1 bomber raid
Aint bout the plans Osama made
Banks get paid off petrol trade
Circulate
Dosey-do
How much cash could a o-z grow?
Til all are fed and all have beds
My skin is Black
My star is red

FBI comin round the outside
Which one of us finna die tonight?
Is we finna fight over crumbs to bite
or make a whole muthafuckin world ignite?
Everybody throw them bows
Right upside your partner's nose
By now you've got bloody clothes
Crabs in the barrel
so the story goes
think of all their savage acts
grabbin scratch from average cats
bureaucrats with strings attached
walk in place

light the match

Two by two
Promenade
Duck from a B-1 bomber raid
Aint bout the plans Osama made
Banks get paid off petrol trade
Circulate
Dosey-do
How much cash could a o-z grow?
Till all are fed and all have beds
My skin is Black
My star is red

Everybody get down low
Bout the level of your toes
These dance moves we usually do
Are not the ones that we have chose
Grab on to that beat and grind
Try your best to stay alive
We can run
We can't hide
Might as well just stay and fight

Two by two
Promenade
Duck from a B-1 bomber raid
Aint bout the plans Osama made
Banks get paid off petrol trade
Circulate
Dosey-do
How much cash could a o-z grow?
Til all are fed and all have beds
My skin is Black
My star is red

# NOBODY MOVES TILL WE SAY GO

RT RAYMOND "BOOTS" RILEY
MUSICIAN & ACTIVIST

RT U.S. POLICE WALK FINE LINE BETWEEN
PROTECT & SERVE AND EXCESSIVE FORCE

Stills from interview with Boots
on RT America.

— NOW LEMME INTRODUCE
MY SLAVE NAME IS RAYMOND RILEY
YOU COULD CALL ME BOOTS
CUZ WE GON BOOT EM OUTTA POWER
THEN SPREAD THE LOOT
FINNA DRIVE THAT FREEDOM TRAIN
NOT RIDE CABOOSE

## NOBODY MOVES TILL WE SAY GO

Tired, broke, and winded
We get low percentage
So, I'm so committed
and I'm so commended
But when I say it's to the death
That's open ended
I might never die
Till bosses is croaked and ended
I might never rhyme unless I put Oakland in it
I might never sleep till this flyer's wrote and printed
This may not be spoken proper
I'm smilin holding choppers
Foot on the coppers
in the photo finish

Nobody moves till we say go
Nobody moves till we say go
Nobody moves till we say go
Nobody moves till we say go

(Go!)
Nobody moves till we say go
(Go! Go!)
Nobody moves till we say go
(Go! Go!)
Nobody moves till we say go
(Go! Go!)
Nobody moves till we say go
(Go! Go!)

In a coat of linen
Not just quotin Lenin
Strike a blow and hit em
Like cobras totin venom
I'm your codefendant
This system's broke and bended
Them millionaires on TV
That's a token image

Plus they're owned and rented
The most we get is a car with spokes
and tinted
Let's get loc'd and win it
We can slow their business
Till their dough diminish
When they meet these demands
We'll be foldin spinach

Nobody moves till we say go
Nobody moves till we say go
Nobody moves till we say go
Nobody moves till we say go

(Go!)
Nobody moves till we say go
(Go! Go!)
Nobody moves till we say go
(Go! Go!)
Nobody moves till we say go
(Go! Go!)
Nobody moves till we say go
(Go! Go!)

Nobody moves till we say go
Nobody moves till we say go
Nobody moves till we say go
Nobody moves till we say go
(Go!)
Nobody moves till we say go
(Go! Go!)
Nobody moves till we say go
(Go! Go!)
Nobody moves till we say go
(Go! Go!)
Nobody moves till we say go
(Go! Go!)

# OTHER SONGS

1.  **SWERVIN'**
2.  **SHAKE IT ON DOWN**

*BRENDAN MURPHY, "JAZZ: THE COUP; STAGING THE COUP," MONTREAL HOUR, JUNE 28, 2007*

Murphy: When Boots answers a question, he answers the shit out of it. Example: I asked why, thematically, he seems to frequently come back to ideas of economics, of capitalism versus socialism:

"An anthropologist will tell you that culture is an outgrowth of people figuring out how to survive and create. To survive under capitalism there are certain things that happen culturally, and these are the problems that we talk about as if we don't know why they're happening.

There's been a whole bunch of killings that happened this year in Oakland, and someone else might say, 'All these young Black folks are going crazy,' either because they have malice towards Black folks or because they refuse to look at the fact that most of the people are getting killed in some kind of dope thing, struggling for money. Why are they struggling for money when we got all this money coming into the Bay Area? They're struggling for money because we have all this money coming into the Bay Area and housing prices are going up, the city is giving corporations tax kickbacks and not making them hire people and prices are going up for rent. So people are desperate. So yeah, I don't bring it back to capitalism, it gets brought back by itself."

# SWERVIN'

"Party promoter days, 1990. Left to right: Mocedes (Tupac's brother—later changed his name to Mopreme and was in *Thug Life*), me, his manager, Earl Jackson (who tried to sign me to a lifetime management contract in which he would own my name and likeness for life)."
—BOOTS